COACHING KIDS FLAG FOOTBALL

COACHING KIDS FLAG FOOTBALL

Danford Chamness

Writers Club Press
San Jose New York Lincoln Shanghai

Coaching Kids Flag Football

Writers Club Press
an imprint of iUniverse, Inc.

For information address:
iUniverse, Inc.
5220 S. 16th St., Suite 200
Lincoln, NE 68512
www.iuniverse.com

ISBN: 0-595-22523-3

Printed in the United States of America

To Larry, Scot, Billy, Nick, Travis, David, Bob, Jack B. and all of the new coaches giving their time and talents to the children who love sports.

Contents

Forward

This book was written expressly for you who are coaching children in Flag Football. We stress how to teach children this complex game and to have fun doing it. The book covers all facets of the game from "how to" throw a ball to strategies and tactics.

When coaching children it should be a fun experience for everyone, for you, for the parents, and most important of all, for the children. As a coach, we cover the teaching attitude and methods. We always keep in mind that these are children, and the game is for the kids and not for the adults. Winning isn't everything, but learning to play well and wanting to win is.

The team is a composite of three important elements. The coaching staff, the parents and the players of the team. Leadership of this composite rests upon the coaching staff. It has the responsibility for directing and maintaining the program from its beginning until its end.

As a coach you are building attitudes and memories with these youngsters that they will carry with them for a lifetime. You give them an identity away from home or school. You have made them a member of a team, and assigned them a responsible position on the team.

This is their first step to independence and self reliance. And you are helping them take that first step. Leading a youngster into his own identity is the birth of their character to come. There is not enough praise that can be given to you for your selfless efforts to train our young people.

I always remain aware that these kids are the hope of all of our tomorrow's. And by doing a good job with them early, you have given more to their future than you realize.

Thank you for your participation.

Acknowledgments

The "National Youth Sports Coaches Association" was developed to train coaches in the techniques and methods of coaching young people. It is coaching specific. I am proud to be a member of this organization, and I highly recommend that you consider becoming one yourself.

NYSCA

National Youth Sports Coaching Association
2050 Vista Parkway, West Palm Beach, FL 33411
(561) 684-1141, (800) 729-2057, Fax (561) 684-2546
E-Mail: nays @ nays.org
Web Site: Intp:/www.nays.org

Becoming a NYSCA certified coach does not indicate that you are qualified in the sense of a paid coach on the high school, college, or professional level. By virtue of your attending the NYSCA Training Certification Program conducted by a qualified Clinician. NYSCA Headquarters certifies that you have been trained in your responsibilities to children in sports specifically.

The City of Burbank, Parks and Recreation Sports Department is an outstanding example of what a well organized group can do. I have had the good fortune of working as a volunteer coach for this department for a number of years. With limited facilities and multiple sports in progress at any one time, they perform pure magic when it comes to scheduling games and practice sessions.

The city through it's meticulous selection of staffing personnel has managed to attract an outstanding number of dedicated people. I thank them for all of the support they have given to the coaches in the coaches efforts to train the children in this community.

Chapter 1

Coaches Corner

So you're ready to coach? Great! This book is dedicated to you and the member's of your team. And as a coach you are more than just a trainer of young athletes in the fine art of this chosen sport, but their mentor and teacher. This carries a lot of responsibility. Not just the idea of building a winning team, but the molding of character and creating a firm foundation of good sportsmanship.

Your own goal should be to have fun teaching these youngsters how to play this most fun form of Football. Make it a point to bring your sense of humor to every practice session or game. Flag Football requires a wide range of skills. It can be a very intricate and complex game played at speed, both in body and mind.

Learn to laugh at yourself and laugh with your team. Have realistic expectations about what your team can accomplish. Share their expectations about what they think they can do. Think more of "we" than "me" and become that winning coach you want to be. All of this effort is for the children, not for the adults.

As their coach, you are responsible for scheduling all practices, getting uniforms, setting game dates, handling the players rotation roster, first aid on the field, player releases and a hundred other details. Don't expect others to appreciate the amount of time and effort you will expend. You are a coach! How well you organize your program is important. You must also have the most current rules publication available to you, because almost every year, some rule changes.

As the coach, you also become the team's trainer. The Training side is when you are teaching the fundamental skills required to play the game, it's the "how to" phase. Under training, you will run practice drills, and give instructions which assist the player in learning "how to". Depending on the age and experience of your new team, the amount of "how to" may vary considerably.

Training for the younger players will require more training time in the basic fundamentals than the older boys. You assess the skill level early on with your team by having them perform the most basic skills required to play the game. Once the teams basic skill level is determined, you either raise or lower the basic skill level of drills to be practiced.

At this point you must develop realistic goals you should hope to achieve with the players. Form a schedule of how and when you should reach a particular goal. Once an overall plan is put together, you are organized. Now you have a means of measuring yourself and your teams success. Having a reference point for achievement is as important to you as it is to the team.

Making your training time count is based upon how you prepare the training program and the amount of detail you put into it. Always have a plan in advance, then follow it. Those youngsters who are slower to learn than the others will of course require more of your personal attention. Give it with a smile.

When we are coaching youngsters, consider boys from 6 to 14 as being in this category. They arrive filled with hope and expectation to improve their skills and to have fun. Don't forget the word play in "play football". Leave the furrowed brow, pulled down mouth and scornful voice at home.

As a coach, you are the leader, trainer, booster, supporter, manager, and a host of many positive things. To be all of that requires constant monitoring of yourself and your reactions. It's a darn tough job. All of us have reflex reactions that at times can be very inappropriate to a situation at hand. Often times holding these in check is difficult if not almost impossible.

Reflex is a conditioned response which can cause us to say or do something we will later regret. Just remember, you can't un-ring the bell. Some people call this overreaction, and it is. That old business about counting to ten first, really holds true, so use it. Like it or not, you are the authority figure. Always conduct yourself as such. Don't smoke, use smokeless tobacco or profanity in front of the team. Set an example you would prefer your son or daughter to have.

Now that I've mentioned your son, it's a good time to consider whether or not you're coaching your own child. If that is the case, there are some guidelines you must consider. Consider first if your child wants you to be his coach. Some children do not want to be coached by a parent because the relation is to close to their daily routine.

Next, review your own reasons and interest for coaching your child. Are you attempting to make him a "star" by giving the child preferential treatment? If that be the case, you're off on the wrong foot. That causes a lot of conflict among other the players on the team, and with their parents. Your child is then subjected to a negative backlash from the other players.

Another problem we run into when coaching our own children is we sometimes expect more from them than their counterparts. This is unfair to the child. Let the child grow at his own rate. Allow him the freedom of being like any other kid on the team. Do not compare your child's accomplishments to those of others.

Don't single your child out for his performance any differently than you do with any other team member. Try to keep the playing field level for all participants. Maintain an even balance when you administer discipline or compliments.

Team Discipline only requires that you be firm and even handed with your directions and your coaching attitude. You are not running a marine barracks. Children lose focus during practice or the drills after a short period of time, that's normal. Don't allow that to irritate you, if it does, give the kids and yourself a break.

Let's talk about the kids for a moment. They are pretty much blank pages for you. They come in a variety of sizes, maturity levels, skill levels, and of playing experience. Some have good hand - eye coordination and some don't. Some may have physical disabilities such as asthma, epilepsy, shortness of breath, hard of hearing, or eye problems which are not obvious by looking at them.

Take any age group, for instance 10 to 11 year old boys, their abilities and sizes will run the gambit. However, there are several common denominators among all youngsters. Their vulnerability, their wanting to please you, and their need for positive reinforcement. Simple achievements build their self esteem. They need you to be their positive booster.

If your kids are lucky, you will create a sports sanctuary where they learn to play the game and have fun doing so. Having fun is the key to good coaching. Make it fun for the players and yourself. No youngster learns well under harsh instruction or by ridicule from either parents or others. Also consider that you have little if any information regarding your wards, other than they are interested in learning to play the game.

Take into account that you know nothing about their outside environment or inner family relationships. Young people have many stressful conditions imposed on them by family expectations, school and their own social group. Some may come from very repressive home environments, some may be mentally and emotionally abused, others can get far worse treatment.

You have no way of knowing what goes on where and with whom in your charge. In pointing this out, I'm urging you to consider first the players need for your booster ability. Treat him fairly and calmly when giving your instructions. Never get into an argument with a child. The moment you do, you have lost. Simply repeat the instruction and move on.

There's a good reason why I've taken this time to point out abuse. Child abuse can be anything from indifference and neglect to murder. Hard words but true. It exists on a wide variety of levels and you as a coach should be aware of it. Take for instance the act of expressing your delight over a players successful performance on the field. High five's, shoulder slaps, hair ruffling or shoulder squeezes are affectionate displays of caring and approval.

And these have a place in the sports arena, they demonstrate acceptance and improve self worth. However, never, and I repeat never pat, rub or touch the kids below the belt. This can easily be misunderstood by him and others.

A player expects fairness from the coach when playing schedules are assigned. No boy wants to be left out while the others are in the game. Players then reflect upon themselves that you don't feel they are good enough to play. And they assume that you, without saying a word have shown your feelings about his playing ability. If he can recognize, and should, that you are being both fair to him as an individual and the team as a whole, you've got a happy camper.

An example of kids thinking can go like this: The boy had a great game, everything he did worked. It was the best he had ever played but the team lost the game. Because the team lost did not make him unhappy because he was happy with how he played. Conversely the boy played a terrible game, nothing worked that he tried but the team won. How do you think he felt about himself? He felt good because the team won.

Winning isn't everything. Losing isn't everything. Playing the game well and wanting to win is everything. Never make too much out of a game lost. Instead have them see it as a learning experience, discuss what adjustments you as a team can make to improve your win/loss performance. Do let the kids know that you are with them and behind them all the way. When you win, you all win, when you lose, you all lose.

You don't have to dictate everything to them. Let them participate in what the team is doing. Encourage the working relationship between the team and you as the coach. Keep an open mind on suggestions and ideas from your team. Let the players arrive at your observation, then confirm it.

Coaching really starts when you begin scrimmages and practice games. And as in a real game, you call a time out, form the team around you and go over what you want to see done. You will have setbacks in the sense that you may have practiced a passing play and the moment the players are in a practice game, it goes out the window.

That is the time when you call a time out, and calmly go over it verbally with the players. When instruction is given during play then it will stick. Conduct your coaching during practice games in the same manner you will use during a league game.

The more advanced and skilled your players or team becomes, the easier your job gets. Let's examine that thought for a moment. When you are coaching a young team that is just developing it's skills, you are looking primarily at the fundamental performance mistakes the players are making. You begin listing in your mind the things you will have to emphasize in training.

The poorest player will set the pace for what you must teach in fundamentals. If you're a hell bent for election, gotta win coach, you may find that this will stress you out. Never point a finger at a player for what he's done wrong, remember that when you do, you have three fingers pointing back at you. You adjust your training.

Here again is that philosophy of don't scold. A player may have made a poor choice in what he did, but scolding won't undo the mistake. Both you and the team must accept the reality that mistakes do happen, and they are okay. You simply emphasize what you would like to have done instead of what was done.

This approach makes the team feel they are supported by you instead of scrutinized by you. Build from the positive things your players are doing well. Ring in the reins a little on the "must win" thinking. Direct the team's efforts and let them experiment and have fun. Having fun and bonding with their teammates will develop the winning team for you and them.

Every team you will coach, whether very young or young adults, will develop a bond among themselves. Their shared experience in working towards a common goal is a coalition of individuals. You will be watching this bond form as they share the playing experience.

Once this has begun to take shape, you must consider more closely how you either correct or reprimand your individual players. From within their bond, you are the outsider. Sure, you are the coach, but not a member of the team. Kids are like rope, you can lead them, pull them along, but you can't push them very well. This brings up fraternization with the players. You are the authority figure, they are not your buddies and don't try to make it so.

Don't start saying to them, "C'mon Buddy you can do it." That's well intended, but not good from the separateness you should maintain as an instructing coach. I don't wish to belabor this point, but refer to them by their names which keeps everything on an even keel. They should refer to you as coach, or mister, or misses and not by your first name. We, as coaches must stand apart in order to get the response we want from them, for them.

During a game, don't make comments to individual players about what they are doing or not doing while they are on the field. When you single out a player, you may embarrass him without meaning to. If you have a player who is not doing what you have requested of him, send in a sub and have him report to you on the side lines. Conduct your business with him privately, then return him to the game.

If the team is not doing what you've asked them to do. Call a time out and review what it is you need them to do. This is conducted in the presence of all team members without anyone being excluded. It's a matter of fairness and consideration. Do corrections in a positive and reinforcing way. No scolding. Explain as clearly as possible the changes you are looking for and do it with a smile.

If you are coaching a team of good players. You don't have to look at basic performance mistakes, because they don't make them. You are now in the process of building teamwork. The longer a good team plays together as a team, the more proficient they become in blocking, running blocks, passing, receiving, hand-offs, etc.. At this coaching level you are teaching your team how to improve and implement strategies and tactics. Therefore during the game, you are looking for the right plays to help them win.

How do you handle an unruly parent who is shouting at the players on the field during the game? At the quarter break or half time break, take the time to thank the parents for their enthusiasm and remind them of their code of responsibility. Do it calmly and quietly and with a smile. If a parent is admonishing his own child, ask him to help the team by taking some of his extra time to work with his kid to improve his performance. Always try to enlist the parent in a positive way to gain the participation you want.

For some unknown reason, parents of players get out of control as a spectator group. Whatever it is about football, parents seem to feel they know more about it than anyone else. You will have them harass you about where their child should be playing on the team. They may never consider that their child has so few skills that you have placed him in a position out of harms way.

After a game, you may have someone call you at home and chew on your ear for some mistake a player made, and it's your fault. The kid would be better off in another position, not the one he is playing. You are going to hear it all. Everyone is your critic. Don't allow those people to undermine your efforts. You aren't doing this for them, you are doing it for the players, and remind yourself of that.

Now that you are the coach, let's look at what this entails other than being the teams trainer and provider. You should keep a first aid kit available at all times during practice and games. Ice packs are almost always in demand for bangs and bruises, with Band-Aid running a close second.

A coach is responsible;

For teaching the fundamentals of the game.
For creating a good learning environment.
For treating each child fairly.
For individual training needs.
For each child's personal safety.
For each child's safety from others abuse.
For setting a good example.
For creating a team environment.
For building players self esteem.
For encouragement and player fun.
For having patience with the children.
For the parents behavior during a game.
For the players behavior during a game.

A coach has the right;

To cooperation from the parents.
To cooperation from the player.
To cooperation from the league.
To bench a player for inappropriate behavior.
To suspend a player from play.
To not accept a problem player on the team.
To assign his players to their positions.
To have adequate practice facilities.
To fairness in scheduling with the league.

One last note, during a league game or when a number of people are in attendance, only allow your team to use the restrooms when all of the players go together. Keep them together at all times for their own individual safety. Make sure all players are picked up after the game or practice and never leave one behind alone. If you have a player who is waiting for someone to pick them up, you wait with them.

Language of the Game

Below are listed the most commonly used terms in football and you should begin early with the youngsters to use them. Vernacular is important to the players and how they converse with each other in their own sports language.

Audible - A change of plays shouted in code at the line of scrimmage by the Quarterback.

Backfield - The area behind the line of scrimmage where the Quarterback and running backs enact their running or passing plays.

Blindside - To block or strip the Quarterbacks flags from behind.

Blitz - A pass rush involving defensive backs individually and linebackers to strip the ball carriers flags before the line of scrimmage may by passed.

Block - In an offensive play, any player on the offense may and will put his body between a defender and the ball carrier. In the case of the linemen, they prevent the defensive line from penetrating the line by shoving their bodies against the defensive linemen.

Bomb - A long pass.

Bootleg - The Quarterback fakes a hand-off, then hides the ball beside his leg or hip and runs around one of his ends.

Bump and Run - A pass defender technique which calls for bumping the intended pass receiver when he comes off the line, then runs with him down field. It's a stalling move to change the pace of play.

Charging - Any attempt by the ball carrier to run over or straight arm the opponent. The ball carrier shall strive to avoid the defense by agility. (No pile-driving)

Clipping - An illegal block caused by throwing the body across the back of an opponent. Clipping usually occurs downfield on punts, kickoffs, and interceptions.

Conversion - A one or two point play after a touchdown by the scoring team. May either be a run or pass play.

Coverage - A pass defense which may also use double coverage on a particular intended pass receiver.

Cross Block - When two offensive linemen change assignments, with each taking the others man on the line. Used to open a hole.

Cutback - A maneuver by a ball carrier reversing his direction against the flow of a play.

Dead Ball - Is when the ball can no longer be advanced and whistled dead by the officials. This also applies to an out of bounds ball.

Defense - Is the team without the ball and whose job it is to prevent the opponent from scoring.

Defensive Backs - Are the men in the backfield such as the cornerbacks and safeties, which is referred to as the secondary.

Dog - Is a term applied to the linebackers during a pass rush play.

Double Coverage - Is when two defensive players cover a receiver.

Double Teaming - Is when two offensive blockers are working against a single defender.

Down - The team in possession has a series of downs numbered 1,2,3, and 4 to advance the ball into each 20-yard zone. When a ball carrier has his flags pulled, he is considered down and the play ends.

Draw - A delayed fake pass play which draws the defense to the backfield for a hand-off play for a running back. The Quarterback may also run, that's a Quarterback sneak.

Drop - Can be the Quarterback moving into the backfield for a pass play or a defensive linebacker who retreats into pass coverage.

Encroachment - A penalty is called when a defender is in the neutral zone when the ball is snapped or makes contact with an opponent before the ball is snapped.

End Around - A variation of a reverse play when the wide receiver is the ball carrier on a sweep.

End Zone - The area, 10 yards deep behind the goal line.

Extra Point - The point or points made from a conversion play.

Fair Catch - An unhindered catch by a receiver of a kickoff or a punt. Once caught, the ball cannot be advanced.

False Start - When an interior offensive lineman moves after the line has been set and the Quarterback is beginning the signal call.

Flag-Guarding or **Warding Off** - The ball carrier may not run with his hands or arms in such a way to prevent the defense from reaching the flag and belt.

Flare Pass - A short pass to a running back usually in the backfield near the sidelines.

Flea-Flicker - A gadget pass play to deceive the defense.

Flood - Putting more receivers into an area than are covered by the defenders in that same area.

Fly Pattern - A long pass pattern where the wide receiver runs full speed downfield. Also a 'go' play.

Forward pass - When the ball is thrown forward across the line of scrimmage to an eligible receiver.

Force - The responsibility of the cornerback or safety to turn a running play towards the middle of the field.

Formation - The alignment of either the offense or defense players on a given play.

Forward Progress - The farthest point reached by the ball carrier before his flags are pulled.

Front - A defensive front or front line made up of the four defensive linemen.

Fumble - Loss of possession of the football by the ball carrier, Quarterback or passer.

Gadget Play - Any trick play to deceive the defense.

Game Plan - A list of strategies and tactics in the form of selected play prior to the games.

Goal Line - The vertical plane between the end zone and field of play that must be crossed or touched to score a touchdown.

Half Time - The intermission between second and third quarters of the game when the team usually rests and discuss plans for the last half of the game.

Hand-off - Giving the ball hand to hand to another player.

Holding - A penalty called for illegal grabbing or grasping another player to prevent them from playing.

Huddle - All players form around the Quarterback behind the scrimmage line to discuss their next play and individual assignments.

Hurdling - An illegal maneuver by the ball carrier to jump over or away from an defender to prevent his flags from being removed.

Illegal Flags - Any flags which have been tied or hooked in any way to hinder the removal of said flags from a player, or flags which have been shortened or altered to hinder removal.

Incomplete Pass - A pass that is not caught or intercepted.

Intentional Grounding - A penalty called when the Quarterback purposely throws the ball away to avoid being sacked for a loss.

Interception - A change of possession when a defensive player catches a pass intended for an offensive player.

Interference - 1.) A penalty called when either an offensive or defensive player interferes with another players opportunity to catch a pass. 2.) In a running play a player other than the ball carrier may run ahead or beside the ball carrier to block defenders away.

Kickoff - The ball is placed on a tee for kicking. The team kicking must remain behind the placement of the ball and cannot move forward until the kicker has made contact with the ball. This puts the ball into play by the receiving team.

Lateral - A toss or pass backwards from the direction of play to another player on the same team.

Lead Block - A block by a running back who blocks in front of another running back who carries the football. He makes contact with the first defender he comes to.

Line Call - A signal called by the offensive center to alert the linemen about their assignments prior to the snap.

Man-to-man - When defense assigns linebackers and defensive backs to potential individual pass receivers for coverage.

Misdirection - Deception by the backfield to mislead defense away from the flow of the play.

Neutral Zone - The space the length of a football between the offense and defensive lines.

Offense - Is the team in possession of the football.

Offside - A penalty called when a player is across the line of scrimmage at the time the ball is snapped.

Onside kick - A short kickoff that carries beyond the 10 yards required to give the kicking team a chance to recover the ball.

Option pass - When the Quarterback has the option to pass to several receivers or when a running back has the option to run or pass and passes.

Option run - When the Quarterback moves down the line and has the option to pass, pitch or run the play.

Outside - When the running play is directed into the area outside of the tackles.

Overshift - When the defensive linemen shift one man over to cover the offensive strong side.

Overtime - An extra period of time to play in which a tie score can be broken.

Pass pattern - A route run by the intended receiver in order to catch the football.

Pass rush - The defensive charge to sack or pressure the Quarterback as he attempts to pass.

Penalty - An infraction of the rules that can cause loss of yardage, loss of down, or loss of a play.

Penalty marker - The yellow flag thrown by the officials to indicate a penalty.

Penetration - Movement of the defensive linemen across the line of scrimmage.

Pitchout - An underhanded toss from the Quarterback to a running back in the backfield.

Play action - When the Quarterback fakes a hand-off to a back, then passes downfield to an intended receiver.

Pocket - A protected area around the Quarterback formed by his blockers so he can make a pass.

Possession - Control of the ball be either an individual or a team.

Punt - A kick used on the fourth down that usually results in a change of possession.

Quarterback sneak - A short yardage gain when the Quarterback runs the ball over the center, or rolls out as if to pass and sweeps around the end.

Quick count - Is an abreviated signal call used to catch the defense off guard.

Read - Used by both offense and defense to "read" the player alignment and adjust their actions accordingly.

Reverse - A running gadget play where the Quarterback will make a hand-off to a running back moving in the opposite direction he has taken. Variations on the theme also include passing plays.

Rollout - When the Quarterback moves sideways in the backfield to set up for a pass.

Rotation - Is shifting zone pass coverage to the left or right.

Sack - When the Quarterback is stripped of his flags behind he line of scrimmage by the opposing team for lost yardage.

Safety - A two point scoring play when the ball handler is stripped of his flags in his own end zone. Also a name assigned to a defensive player in his own backfield.

Scramble - When the Quarterback runs to avoid being sacked.

Screen pass - When the ball is thrown to a running back or wide receiver behind the line of scrimmage. Usually a delayed pass play to deceive the defense.

Scrimmage line - An imaginary line from the sidelines through the center of the football before it is snapped. It is the line from which a play begins.

Secondary - The defensive backfield and the pass coverage players.

Shift - The movement of offensive or defensive linemen prior to a snap.

Shotgun - An offensive alignment where the Quarterback takes the ball from the center at five to seven yards behind the line.

Signals - Are codes called by both offense and defense prior to the snap of the football. On offense it is the Quarterback and on defense it is by the middle linebacker.

Snap - The passing action of the football to the Quarterback, punter, or holder to begin the play action. Also called a hike.

Snap count - Is the signal on which the ball will be snapped.

Special teams - The offensive and defensive units used during kickoffs, punts, and extra points.

Spot - The placement of the football after a play or a penalty by the referee.

Spot of enforcement - The spot from which a penalty or foul is marked off, it varies depending with the situation.

Spot pass - A pass pattern depending on timing and coordination, where the Quarterback will be passing to a spot on the field and the receiver must run into that spot for a reception.

Strong side - Is the side of the offense away from center with the most players aligned.

Sweep - A run around one end.

Time out - A halt to the game action called by either team or the referee. Each team is allowed to call for a time out for team instruction or assignment changes.

Touch back - When a ball is whistled dead on or behind the offensive goal line. An example is the football going into the end zone on a kickoff and placed at the 20 yard line.

Touchdown - A six point scoring play when the offense crosses the other teams goal line with the ball in their possession.

Weak side - The side of the offensive line to one side of the center with a fewer number of players.

Zone - An assigned area of pass defense.

These terms we've listed above are only a part of the large vocabulary of the game. Regulation football played in high school or college or the NFL, has a variety of play names and terms to many to ever be considered here. We've feather dusted the most common terms you will find, but they belong to this sport and you.

Chapter 2

Players Bench

Let's begin with what kids are about when they get together. It is about having fun and playing with each other. They mingle and mix and show off for each other. They chatter with and challenge one another in their activities. When all of the boys are members of a single team, the taunting doesn't erupt into hostility, it is a form of bonding. Being together is a joy which is hard to define to an adult, but the kids all feel it.

The youngsters coming into the football program want a place where they can play with others like themselves and practice whatever skills they have. Usually they arrive with a great deal of interest about the sport and an attitude about their own ability. However the majority of youngsters are shy and don't want to be singled out to do things which they may not do well.

Yet, they all want to fit in with the others in your program. Each player wants an opportunity to do what he does best, or thinks he does best. He expects the coach to recognize his skills and abilities and instruct him in how to improve them. He expects to be included in all of the activities fairly.

It is my opinion that every player believes that he can play any position on the team and expects the opportunity to do so. And they should be given that opportunity until they discover for themselves where they are most comfortable playing. Comfort will come from the success they have in a given assignment.

Players prior to the age of puberty are looking at the sport for fun. Players after reaching puberty look at the sport as a way to establish an identity. Young players share interest and involvement. Older players share the same interest and involvement but bring another dimension when seeking identity. In overall respect, all players are wanting to have fun with the game and all of them should.

All players regardless of age seek leadership from adults and coaches. All players want acceptance and recognition. All players want to play in the game. Some boys are seeking a haven away from their outside environment. To find a place where they fit. A player expects fairness from the coach when playing schedules are assigned.

No player wants to either be made the subject of scrutiny nor to be ignored. During a practice or a game, he expects leadership from the coach in how to best play the game. He is more than willing to follow directions if they are explained in a way which he can understand. Most players feel that if they work hard in practice, do their best as directed, should have the right to play in the game.

This is a players fairness doctrine that should be adhered to. No player is looking to be the fair hair boy, and resents it if there appears to be someone who is. Boys in this sport find their own place among their peers. It is a place of comfort for them to play from in the team.

All youngsters are sensitive to correction and how corrections are made. No player on your team wants to be scolded, talked to abusively or harshly corrected for whatever mistake he makes. He does not expect to be ordered around like a small child or treated as if he's not good enough to play with the other players.

Player's Rights & Responsibilities:

To fairness and respect.
To have fun learning and playing.
To not be ridiculed or harshly scolded.
To make mistakes without punishment.
To a fair amount of playing time in the game.
To encouragement for effort.
To protection from abuse by others.
To a safe environment.

A player is responsible;

For attending practices.
For attending the game.
For trying To make a learning effort.
For good conduct on the field.
For cooperating with others.
For following directions.
For letting the coach know if he is ill.
For staying with the team at all times.
For asking permission to leave the game.

Chapter 3

Parents Expectations

Parents expect their children to be taught how to play their game of choice while having fun. They expect the coach to be thoughtful, considerate, kind and fair to their prize possession. Parents who involve their young children in sports do so for a variety of reasons. First they want their children to have fun in sports, and group activities.

Parents want their youngsters to acquire self esteem and confidence and to learn the values of good sportsmanship. They want their kids to build a network of friends and enjoy an activity which in the future may guide them away from trouble. All of this is as it should be, and it is also the coach's focus as well.

Parents sometimes have unrealistic expectations about their child's ability to master the basics of the game. They often expect to much from their youngsters. These expectations should be tempered with the realization that they are only children. We have a situation where kids are playing at grown up games. Some children will learn quicker than others and some will be slower than the rest. So what! Parents must let the kids have their play time.

All parents want their children to perform well. When they don't, they get disappointed with their children, the team and the coaches. Not a good thing to have happen. They should never be unhappy over kids trying to play this game as best they can. When the parent gets unhappy with their child's, or the children's performance, their kid feels defeated by not living up to their expectations of him. This spoils it for the child.

Some things a parent should never do.

Never ridicule one of the team members lack of ability to play well to your child. By bad rapping another players deficiencies to your child, only makes him defensive about "his" team.

Never take your coach to task in front of the team. You may not know all you should about either playing the game or coaching it. Never assume that you know why a coach is doing what he is doing.

Never scold your child in the presence of the team either at a practice or a game for what you feel he did or did not do.

Never insist that your child should play if he is ill or suffering from an injury. No child should be requested to play if he is in pain. It could result in long term injury which we all wish to avoid.

During a game, never shout and demean another team and its players by completely forgetting that the other team is made of children the same as your own.

During a game, don't take the officials to task over a call or calls that he has made. It will not change the officials decision and only reflects upon your team and your child.

A parent has the right;

To share in their child's training experience.
To encourage their child and the team.
To be concerned about their child's safety.
To see their child treated fairly.
To want their child's self esteem to grow.

To expect the coach to teach sportsmanship.
To expect the coach to set a good example..

A parent has the responsibility;

To get their child to practice on time.
To get their child to the game on time.
To notify the coach of illness.
To participate with team activities.

A parent has the responsibility for picking up their child after a practice or a game. If that is not possible, then advise the coach of who will be recovering the player so the coach will know.

Chapter 4

Rostering a Team

All federations involved with youth Flag Football operates pretty much the same. We will adhere to the rules and regulations set forth by one of the nations premier municipal organizations with a long and successful career in bringing organized Flag Football to the young people in their own community.

For situations not specifically covered in these rules, the current edition of the National High School Federation will serve as standard rules.

I would like to suggest that you roster your team with children from the same grade level. Don't mix and match. If it's all third graders or all fourth graders that's fine. Human nature has a built in sorting machine that sets a pecking order. We don't want to create a form of segregation based on school grade level identification.

This may not be voiced by your players to you, but it will be there working against you. Think about it, before you do it. At least attempt to have a homogenous team. Each player then is truly among his own peers.

Roster Rules:

A roster must contain the name, address, city, phone number, signature, school, birth date, and grade of each player and parents signature.

1. **Get a list of players from the Sports Office waiting list.**
   a. If you have one player or a group, have them help find new players to join the team Never ask a child to quit his/her team to join yours. Names obtained from the Sports Office will be used first.
   b. We suggest coaches follow minimum/maximum guidelines set up in the rules for roster formation.
   c. If you want to pick up a team from a specific school, have the players do "scouting" for you. Be sure to check with the principal of the school before going onto the playground.
2. **Pick up Manager information from the Sports Office and read all the material.**
3. **Contact the players and let them know they are on your team.**
   a. Be sure to give them your name and phone number. Have them write it down.
   b. For younger players, give the information to the parents.
   c. Be sure to have them call you if they decide not to play.
   d. Let the Sports Office know if any child is not going to be on your team.
4. **Call a meeting of all children and their parents.**
   a. Advise them to bring money for the team entry fee (insurance, etc.) and team equipment if needed.
   b. Ask for parental help if needed or desired and choose an emergency manager in case you can't make it to a game. Get fathers and mothers to help coach the team if possible.
   c. Set up practice times convenient to you and your team.

d. Many teams are commercially sponsored. Find out if any parent would be willing to sponsor or work for a company that would be willing to pick up the cost of sponsoring your team. It is a tax write-off for businesses that sponsor teams.

5. **Pick a team name.**

6. **Decide on team uniform.**

    a. Teams may choose what type of uniforms they want. Football pants are encouraged, however shorts may be worn. Check equipment.

    b. Rubber cleats are allowed. Steel cleats are forbidden; the multi-purpose sport shoe is recommended.

7. **Discuss philosophy of the league.**

    a. Discuss the Player Code of Conduct.

    b. Discuss the player responsibility to the team.

    c. Emphasize Sportsmanship.

8. **Purchase equipment.**

    a.. Balls. Check with the Sports Office for the type of ball required for your league.

    b. The accepted footwear will be rubber cleats or tennis shoes. No steel cleats, street shoes, or playing barefoot is allowed.

    c. All players MUST wear a protective mouth piece.

    d. Team members must wear jerseys of the same color with numbers on the back and must be worn so as not to impede the pulling of the flags. Shirts must be tucked in or hang no longer than top of player's abdomen. Reversible jerseys are preferred with one side being white.

    e. Practice flags and plastic field cones.

Chapter 5

Managing A Team

All federations involved with youth Flag Football operates pretty much the same. We will adhere to the rules and regulations set forth by one of the nations premier municipal organizations with a long and successful career in bringing organized Flag Football to the young people in their own community.

For situations not specifically covered in these rules, the current edition of the National High School Federation will serve as standard rules.

I. MANAGER'S AND COACH'S RESPONSIBILITY

A. All managers and coaches must be in good standing with their Athletic Federation.

B. Managers are directly responsible to the Athletic Federation and the Park and Recreation Department for league fees, rosters, team business, team eligibility and conduct of players, coaches, parents, and spectators.

C. Managers are responsible for initiating Players' Medical Benefit Fund forms and accident forms being filled out and returned to the Sports Office.

D. Managers must report all accidents to the field supervisor at the time of the accident so that a Park, Recreation Department accident form may be completed.

E. Coaches must keep their spectators and players between the 20 yard markers when on the sidelines. Coaches may not go on the field unless given permission by the officials. (In the 3/4 grade league, one coach will be allowed on the field during the game as long as he does not hinder the officials or hold up play.)

F. All teams must have a responsible adult at all games and practices.

G. Team managers will be responsible for keeping their teams off the general playing area until the conclusion of the preceding game.

H. Managers are responsible for the proper care and immediate return of all Parks and Recreation Department equipment and all sponsor's uniforms and equipment.

I. Managers are responsible for the conduct of their team's spectators and will take all necessary steps to inform them of the rules, purposes and philosophy of the Flag Football Program. Discretion of the referee or the Sports Office Staff will be used to handle a situation if needed.

J. Managers must inform their players to report all accidents to the park supervisor at the time they occur so that a Recreation Department Accident Form may be completed.

K. Managers, coaches and spectators may not smoke on the playing field or on the sidelines.

M. All coaches shall be required to comply with the requirements established by the Park and Recreation Department for background checks for volunteers.

N. If a manager or coach is apt to be late, arrangements should be made for another responsible adult to have the line-up and the equipment in order to start the game on time.

O. Coaches will refrain from verbally coaching their players in a negative manner while they are on the field. Discretion of the referee or the Sports Office Staff will be used to handle the situation.

P. Spectators may not verbally coach from the bleachers, sidelines, opposite side of the field, or in any way interfere with the game.

Q. Managers and coaches signatures must appear on the official team roster.

R. Each team will be allowed one coach or manager designated to speak or discuss with the officials.

The rules of the National High School Federation Associations shall be enforced unless amended. Situations not specifically covered in these league rules shall be left to the discretion of the Burbank Athletic Federation Board of Directors and Sports Office staff.

II. PLAYERS ELIGIBILITY

A. All players must be in good standing with the Athletic Federation.

B. A player is not eligible until his signature appears on a team's roster. PENALTY for not rostering a player, FORFEITURE of all games in which he played illegally and suspension of player.

C. A Player may play above his grade grouping but not below.

D. 7-9 grade teams will be allowed no more than 2 ninth graders. (Exceptions will be based on ninth grade sign ups.)

E. A player's residency will be established as of the first day of practice round for the league. Eligibility established at that date will stand for the remainder of the season.

F. A player can play for only one Flag Football team under the jurisdiction of the Athletic Federation.

1. A player may not play in a lower classification than he was originally in after league play starts, except with the League Director's approval.

2. A player must appear in three league games to be eligible for league play-offs.

3. No additions can be made to the roster after the beginning of the second round of league play except in cases of emergency, and these must be approved by the League Director.

TEAM CLASSIFICATION

A. Team grouping is determined by the highest grade represented by any boy on the team. Teams will be classified according to grade.

B. Grade divisions will be 3/4, 5/6, and 7-9.

G. Waiver

1. After the deadline for the roster, a player may be added only by waiver.

   a. Forms may be obtained from the Sports Office and must be filled out completely and signed by the League Director before they are taken out to be signed by the other managers.

   b. As soon as the waiver is received and endorsed by the Sports Office, the player will be notified and immediately made eligible to play. Only members of the Sports Office staff may receive applications or waivers for transfers.

   c. New pitchers must be approved by the Sports Office, and waivers must be signed by each manager of that league. Exception: In the top division of each age group, any rostered player may pitch (except nonresident players).

   d. The waiver procedure is valid only through the first half of the season. No waivers will be issued during the second half.

   e. **WARNING**: Any manager who is asked by another manager to sign a waiver is free to sign or not sign. The signature of the

Sports Office staff member on the form does not constitute approval of the waiver.

H. Release

1. A player desiring a release must have a waiver form filled out, must secure the signature of the releasing manager, and must be authorized by the Sports Office before signing up with another team.

2. A manager may drop a player from his roster only by writing a letter subject to approval by the Sports Office.

III. TEAM ELIGIBILITY

A. No team shall bear the name of, or any trade name of, any alcoholic or tobacco products. All team names including those incorporating a sponsor name are subject to approval of the League Director.

B. All teams must have league fees paid and rosters submitted by the dates set by the Sports Office.

C. Rosters

1. A roster of players must be in the Sports Office by the specified date in the season. Rosters not turned in by this date will automatically release any player of his signature, and upon application to the Sports Office, a player may join any team that wants him.

2. The roster may not contain more than 15 players unless by special arrangement with the League Director.

3. A roster must contain the name, address, city, zip code and phone number, signature, school, birth date and grade of each player and a parent signature.

4. In any case where a participant has deliberately falsified his record, those games in which he participated shall be forfeited and the player suspended.

5. All rostered players must live or attend school in Burbank at the start of the season. **Exception:** Each team will be allowed to have two nonresident players provided that the player's parent/guardian is an active coach or manager or participates actively in a team organizational role as approved by the Sports Office. This nonresident player must be noted as such on the roster. A player's residency will be established as of the first day of practice round for the league. Eligibility established at that date will stand for the remainder of the season.

6. Any player that puts his signature on two different rosters shall automatically be suspended until his case is brought before the Burbank Athletic Federation.

7. All rosters and waivers are subject to approval by the Athletic Federation Director with intentions of maintaining the league on an even competitive scale.

8. Managers must sign their rosters or waivers to certify that all ages and grades are correct.

9. Managers are responsible for the eligibility of all names of personnel on his roster.

IV. PARK GROUND RULES

All ground rules will be explained by the referees and/or park supervisor before game time. These will become the official ground rules for the game. Any situations not covered are left to the discretion of the referee. It would be in the manager's best interest to ask pertinent questions during the pre-game meeting.

V. INSURANCE/PLAYERS MEDICAL BENEFIT FUND

All teams in the Hap Minor Leagues have included as a part of their league fees a membership in the Players' Medical Benefit Fund.

A. Claim procedure

1. Injured boy or team manager must obtain a claim form from the Sports Office.

2. A complete City Accident form must be filled out and filed.

3. Team manager must sign the form and return it to the Sports Office for forwarding to the claims office.

4. Players pay their own medical expenses and are reimbursed up to $500 per year.

5. Detailed instructions are available from the Sports Office.

VI. SELECTING A CHAMPION/DETERMINING A WINNER

A. Refer to the "Determining A Champion" letter sent to the managers at the beginning of league play.

VII.SPORTSMANSHIP

A. Yelling at the opposing team will not be tolerated. No negative yelling will be allowed, including the harassment of the officials or opposing players. One warning will be issued. After that, the game will be subject to forfeiture. Parents, coaches and managers are expected to serve as good examples.

B. No unison yelling will be allowed.

C. Good sportsmanship will be expected at all times, under all circumstances. This includes spectators and participants showing good sportsmanship.

D. Encourage your own players.

Chapter 6

Rules of the Game

The game is played with a regulation football, youth or intermediate by two teams of eight players. The team in possession has a series of downs numbered 1,2,3, and 4 to advance the ball into each 20-yard zone. Points are scored by a touchdown, a successful try for conversion point(s), or a safety.

Flag Football is not tackle football or power football. The defense and offense strive by speed, quickness, and agility to defeat the opponent. A basic concept of the game is for the ball carrier to avoid bodily contact with the defensive players. Likewise the defensive players should go for the ball carrier's flags. The defense MUST play the flag and not the football when pursuing a ball carrier.

A. Field Dimensions: For 5/6 and 7-9 grades the playing area length is 80 yards, divided into four, 20-yard zones. The end zones shall be 10 yards in depth. The width is 40 yards, space permitting. For 3/4 grade, playing area is sixty yards, divided into three, 20 yard zones. The end zones are 10 yards in depth The width shall he 40 yards, space permitting.

B. The game will consist of 4 quarters, each of ten minutes duration running time. The clock will Stop only for time outs, except the last two minutes of the second and fourth quarters when stop clock rules will be used.

C. Each team will be allowed 5 time-outs per game with no more than 3 being allowed in any one half. During time-outs, ONE coach may go onto the field and huddle with his team or he may call ONE player to the sideline.

D. There will be a one minute time-out between quarters and a five minute time-out at half time.

E. At least seven legal rostered players must be present and ready to play at game time. If not enough players are present the opposing team shall win by forfeit. A team which forfeits a game without giving the Sports Office 48 hours notice shall be responsible for both the officials' fees, payable to the Sports Office before their next game.

F. Substitutions are free and unlimited. However, substitutions must be made so that play is not delayed.

G. All players must play the equivalent of at least one quarter or more in every game. Exceptions will he allowed for players missing practice unexcused or for other disciplinary reasons. Players who will not participate for the required time must he reported to the game officials before the game.

H. Scoring shall he according to high school rules with the exceptions of no field goals and the choice of one or two point conversions. One point conversion: The ball shall be placed on the 2 yard line for the attempt. Two point conversion: The ball shall be placed on the 5 yard line.

I. Radical score: A 30 point lead after the end of third quarter will constitute a radical score.

Radical score games will be continued only at the request of both the losing and winning team.

EQUIPMENT:

A. The accepted footwear will be rubber cleats or tennis shoes. No steel cleats, street shoes, or playing barefoot is allowed.

B. All players MUST wear a protective mouth piece. Players found in the game without a mouth piece will be removed until he gets one and the team will be penalized 5 yards.

C. Protective equipment is not allowed unless approved by the Sports Office. Officials may request the immediate removal of any equipment.

D. Team members must wear jerseys of the same color with numbers on the back and must be worn so as not to impede the pulling of the flags. Shirts must be tucked in or hang no longer than top of player's abdomen.

E. Teams must be able to provide T-shirts or jerseys opposite their main jersey color in order to avoid teams wearing the same color jersey when competing against each other. Reversible jerseys are preferred with one side being white.

F. Football pants are encouraged. Shorts may be worn, but may not have belt loops, pockets and must fit appropriately (not too baggy). "Too Baggy" will be held to the discretion of the officials and Sports Office Staff.

G. Pull away flag belts, with three flags will be used in all games and will he provided by the Sports Office for games.

H. 3/4 and 5/6 grades shall use the Junior or Youth size football; 7-9 grades shall use the regulation Intermediate football. Sports Office will provide the ball for all games.

PUTTING THE BALL INT.O PLAY

Field Dimensions: For 5/6 and 7-9 grades the playing area length is 80 yards, divided into four, 20-yard zones. The end zones shall be 10 yards in depth. The width is 40 yards, space permitting. For 3/4 grade, playing area is sixty yards, divided into three, 20 yard zones. The end zones are 10 yards in depth The width shall he 40 yards, space permitting.

A. The winner of the pregame toss may choose either to kick or receive or which goal to defend.

B. The loser of the toss shall have the remaining choice.

C. At the beginning of the Second half. the loser of the pregame toss shall have the three choices to choose from.

D. Kicking team shall kickoff from the 20 yard line in the 3/4 grade division and from the 30 yard line in the 5/6 grade and 7/9 grade divisions. These lines will act as the kickoff teams restraining line.

E. The midfield line shall act as the restraining line for the receiving team.

F. On kickoffs. the kicking team may use any formation as long as the entire team is behind their restraining line and in bounds. The receiving team may use any formation as long as the entire team is behind their restraining line and at least 3 players are within five yards of the restraining line.

G. A kickoff must travel at least 10 yards to be legal unless touched by a receiving team member. If the ball does not travel the required distance, but stays in-bounds, the receiving team may take the Ball where it stopped or force the kicking team to kick over at 5 yards back.

H. When a Kickoff goes out of bounds after going ten yards, the receivers may take the ball at the spot (if touched by a receiver, the ball is automatically placed where it went out), or take the ball 5 yards behind their restraining line.

I. On punts, the receiving team must have five players on the line of scrimmage.

J. When a punt goes out of bounds the receiving team shall take possession at that yard line.

K. If any kickoff or punt enters the end Zone, whether touched by the receiving team or not, it is automatically dead and is put into play on the 20 yard line. No running kicks out of the end Zone.

L. On both kickoffs and punts, the kicking team may recover a kick but may not advance the ball.

M. There shall he no offensive plays through the interior line. The game officials will establish a zone 5 yards wide (2 1/2 yards on each side of the ball) through which no plays may be run.

This will include reverses and delays. Penalty for running through the middle will be automatic dead ball, at the line of scrimmage and loss of down.

N. All players are eligible pass receivers, any formation is allowed and direct runs by the quarterback are permitted.

O. Only one player may be put into motion before the ball is snapped.

P. Every player must take part in the huddle, however a huddle is not required. No player may leave his team's huddle in advance of his teammates. The sleeper play is illegal.

Q. If any portion of the football crosses a first down zone line, the next forward zone line will be used for attaining a first down.

R. There will be a 25 second limit to each huddle. The Count shall begin when the official places the ball, and end when the ball is centered.

S. The fair catch signal is permissible.

T. The ball becomes dead when the ball carrier has his flags pulled. If the ball carrier loses his flags inadvertently, the ball will be declared dead when the ball Carrier is touched by a defensive player.

U. Should a defensive player pull the flags of a receiver before the Ball is in his possession, the following will apply.

1. Ball dropped - 12 yard penalty from line of scrimmage.

2. Ball Received - 12 yard penalty from point reception. If in the officials view, the receiver would have scored, a touchdown may be awarded.

V. It is illegal for a player to leave his feet to block.

BLOCKING - The offense may contact opponents with their arms provided:

A. The elbows are entirely outside the shoulders.

B. The hands are closed or cupped with the palms not facing the opponent.

C. The forearms are approximately parallel to the ground, in the same horizontal plane and extended not more than 45 degrees from the body. The blocker's hands may not be locked nor may the blocker throw, or flip his elbow or forearm so that it is moving faster than his shoulders at the time of contact. The block must be between the waist and the shoulder of the opponent with at least one foot in contact with the ground at the time of the block.

BALL THEFT - In flag football the defense must play the flag of the ball carrier. To attempt to strip the ball is unsportsman like conduct.

CLIPPING - It is clipping to block an opponent from the blind side.

CHARGING - Any attempt by the ball carrier to run over or straight arm the opponent. The ball carrier shall strive to avoid the defense by agility. (No pile-driving)

DIVING - Ball carrier may not dive to advance the ball for extra yardage. Defense may not dive (outstretched and feet leave the ground) for the flag.

FLAG-GUARDING or **WARDING OFF** - The ball carrier may not run with his hands or arms in such a way to prevent the defense from reaching the flag.

ILLEGAL FLAGS - Any flags which have been tied or hooked in any way to hinder the removal of said flags from a player, or flags which have been shortened or altered to hinder removal.

OFFSIDE - When a player is on the opponent's side of the scrimmage line when the snap is imminent.

PUSHING - To use hands, arms, or any part of the body to attempt to stop a ball carrier or force him out of bounds.

ROUGHING THE PASSER - Any contact with a passer's arm before or during the release of the ball. In flag football the defense is to play the flag, not the ball. When the defense is within three feet of the passer they must go for the flag. Contact after the release of the ball is unnecessary roughness.

SHIFTING - Ends and backs after setting a hand down at the start of a play may shift, interior lineman may not.

TIMING OF GAME

The game shall he divided into four quarters of equal time as pre-scribed in the league rules.

1st Quarter - Clock Time 1 Minute Intermission.

2nd Quarter - Clock Time except last two minutes

<u>5 Minute Half Time</u>.

3rd Quarter - Clock Time 1 Minute Intermission.

4th Quarter - Clock Time except last two minutes.

During clock time the game clock will he stopped only for a team time-out, an injury time-out, or an official's time-out. During the last two minutes of each half the clock will stop for:

1) any time-out.

2) ball goes out of bounds.

3) an incomplete pass.

4) a penalty.

5) a first down (clock starts on "ready to play").

6) a score.

7) change of team possession (clock starts on "ready to play").

8) declared punts.

FLAG FOOTBALL PENALTIES

* Loss of down.

Automatic first down.

+ If penalty occurs behind the spot where the ball is whistled dead penalty is enforced from the point gained.

xx If in the opinion of the game officials, the ball carrier would have scored, a touch down may be awarded.

INFRACTION	PENALTY	LOCATION
Offside (encroachment)	5 yards	line of scrimmage
Backfield in motion	5 yards	line of scrimmage
Illegal procedure	5 yards	line of scrimmage
Illegal flags	12 yards	line of scrimmage
Up the center	dead ball	* line of scrimmage
Delay of game	5 yards	line of scrimmage
Intentional grounding	5 yards	* point of infraction
Defensive holding	12 yards	+ point of infraction
Tackling	12 yards	point of infraction
Clipping	12 yards	point of infraction
Unnecessary roughness	12 yards	+ point of infraction
Roughing the Kicker	12 yards, 1st	Down + line of scrimmage
Roughing the Passer	12 yards, 1st	Down # line of scrimmage
Pass interference	12 yards, 1st	down # line of scrimmage
Warding off	12 yards	* point of infraction
Piledriving	12 yards	* point of infraction
Unsportsmanlike conduct	12 yards	after spotting the ball
Illegal forward pass	5 yards	line of scrimmage
Leaving feet to block	12 yards	point of infraction
Leaving feet to pull flags	5 yards	point of infraction
Offensive holding	12 yards	point of infraction
Punting -10 second violation	5 yards	* line of scrimmage
Pushing the ball carrier	12 yards	xx* point of infraction
Premature flag pulling	12 yards	xx* point where ball is dead.
Missing mouthpiece	5 yards	line of scrimmage

Chapter 7

The Teams

The teams are Offense and Defense comprised with eight players per team. Seven are required for play.

Offense: (8) Players.

The **Center** is assigned responsibility for hiking or snapping the ball to the Quarterback when the play is initiated, and moved upon the Quarterbacks called signal. He also blocks the nose tackle from the opposing team.

Guards and Tackles flank the Center on either side. From left to right would be Tackle, Guard, Center, Guard, Tackle. In turn they become **Left Tackle, Left Guard, Center, Right Guard, Right Tackle.** This is called the *interior line* and will either work together to open a hole in the opposing line for the runner to run through, or hold the line closed to allow the **Quarterback** to pass or start a running play.

The **backfield** is made up of the **Quarterback** and two **Wide Receivers.** These become the action players which trigger the play. In Flag Football, any lineman may also be assigned as a pass receiver. However, only the backs can initiate and perform the running plays.

Defense: (8) Players.

The defensive line is made up of four players, and this is called the *front four*. The line consists of two Tackles and two Ends. They are called the **Defensive Tackles** and **Defensive Ends**. These players are usually the larger players and their jobs are (1) to stop the running attack and (2) rush the passer.

The **Linebackers** (2 or 3) line up just back of the front four, and fill the gaps between players on the front line. They are the defensive teams version of the "handymen". They must pursue running plays, drop back and defend against passes <u>or</u> disrupt pass plays with all out rushes from positions called dogs & blitzes.

The **Cornerbacks** and **Safeties**, also called defensive backs, operate in the area called the secondary. They are required to have the speed to strip the flag from the opposing teams runner and be quick enough to interrupt or intercept their opponents pass plays. If a pass play is completed, they must be able to run down the receiver and strip his flags.

Offensive Line: T= (2)Tackle G= (2)Guard Ct= Center

Backfield: WR= (2)Wide Receiver/Tight End QB=Quarterback

Defensive Line: DE= (2) Defensive Ends DT= (2) Defensive Guards

Defensive Backfield: LB= (2/3) Line Backers Sf= (1/2) Safety or Cornerbacks.

OFFENSE:

The offensive plays will be called by the Quarterback during the huddle after each play. All members of the team shall take their place in the huddle as required by rules. Whenever the whistle is blown declaring the play over, the team will quickly come to huddle for instructions. No Coach will be allowed on the field except during time outs. <u>The exception to this rule is 3/4 grades.</u>

The Quarterback may receive next play instructions by signals from the Coach at the sidelines. During the Quarter time out given as one minute, the Quarterback may come to the sidelines for play discussion.

DEFENSE:

The Defensive line shall be put into place by the Middle Linebacker whose responsibility is to place the Defense as quickly as possible after the previous play has been declared dead by the referee. The Front Four will penetrate shutting down the play as quickly as possible. The Middle Linebacker has three choices for defense. The Front Four, the Three-Four and the Colt 3-3-2. Best defense to date has been the Front Four, Left & Right Linebacker, with Middle and Safety playing secondary.

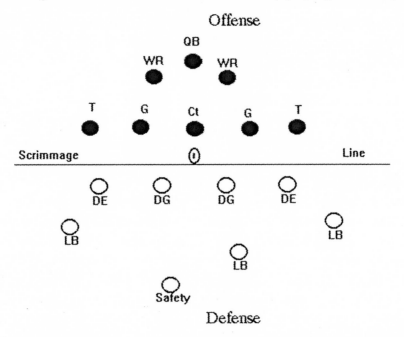

This is considered the traditional setup for Flag Football formations, but it's not one you should get stuck with. While it may work well for a lineman going out as a receiver and the backs block for the passer, it also gives up several yards to defensive advantage.

It will also pull the running back to far from the line for a man in motion hand-off play to pick up his coverage to make it around the end of the line. Only the running backs and the Quarterback can run the ball in Flag Football. If it's a Quarterback run around the end, it does put his two backs in good blocking position as they make the sweep with the Quarterback around the end.

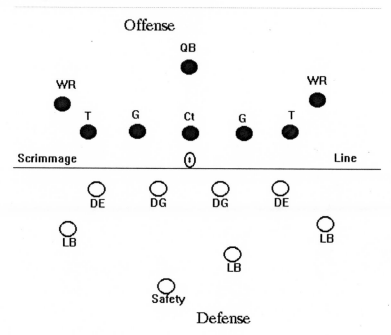

These two illustrations are intended to acquaint you with the basic formations you will be confronted with in this game. They also point out where your options are with the Wide Receivers. Depending on how you place your Wide Receivers, it will allow them to receive lateral passes, which in turn they may pass to a receiver or return it to the Quarterback who may run or pass to a receiver down field.

Player position selection is important to get the greatest performance based on physical attributes. Also in concert with the physical side, is desire to play, attention to the game, mental quickness, desire to excel, and to remain alert at all times when on the field.

Center. The lineman who snaps the ball to the Quarterback upon a pre determined call signal. He should be one of the larger players who can work as a line blocker to hold out defensive penetration. He must also have quickness and good pass receiving abilities. A lot of pass plays are short hitches to the Center for short yardage.

Guard. This position favors the larger players who can work as a line blocker to hold out defensive penetration. He must also have quickness and good pass receiving abilities. Often this player must work with the tackle next to him to open a hole in the line for a running play to be made.

Tackle. Size would be a big help here, but quickness to bump and run as a receiver does just as much. He must be able to run well in order to escort and block a running play around his end, and to be a good pass receiver. He will often be assigned a streak play where he is the receiver.

Wide Receiver. Tall would be a plus, but a good runner with good skills in pass receiving should be a must. Added to that would be his ability to throw a pass. During a play, he may receive a lateral pass and in turn throw it down field to a receiver. He must have many of the skills you will find in the Quarterback.

Quarterback. The man who is in charge of the offense. He calls the plays and is the primary passer and ball handler. He can exercise the option of passing or running the ball by reading the defense.

Player numbers:

All NFL players are numbered according to their positions.

1 - 19   Quarterbacks and Kickers
20-49   Running Backs and Defensive Backs
50-59   Centers and Linebackers
60-79   Defensive Linemen and Interior Offensive Linemen
80-89   Wide Receivers and Tight Ends
90-99   Defensive Linemen

Chapter 8

BASICS OF THE GAME

Flag football is played with 16 players on the field. Offense consists of 8 players and defense consists of 8 players. It is configured more like Arena Football than regulation football. In Flag Football you do not have halfbacks, fullbacks or typical tight ends. Instead you use what is called wide receivers who can run the ball or go out for pass receptions. Any player on offense is an eligible pass receiver, only the wide receivers or running backs and the quarterback can run the ball.

Putting the ball into play

The winner of the pregame toss may choose either to kick or receive or which goal to defend. The loser of the toss shall have the remaining choice. At the beginning of the Second half. the loser of the pregame toss shall have the three choices to choose from. Kicking teams shall kickoff from the 20 yard line in the 3/4 grade division and from the 30 yard line in the 5/6 grade and 7/8 grade divisions. These lines will act as the kickoff teams restraining line.

Field Dimensions: For 5/6 and 7-8 grades the playing area length is 80 yards, divided into four, 20-yard zones. The end zones shall be 10 yards in depth. The width is 40 yards, space permitting. For 3/4 grade, playing area is sixty yards, divided into three, 20 yard zones. The end zones are 10 yards in depth The width shall he 40 yards, space permitting.

The midfield line shall act as the restraining line for the receiving team. On kickoffs. the kicking team may use any formation as long as the entire team is behind their restraining line and in bounds. The receiving team may use any formation as long as the entire team is behind their restraining line and at least 3 players are within five yards of the restraining line.

Kicking

In flag football, there are only two kinds of kicks. One is from a tee which supports the ball upright on one end for a **kickoff** and the other is a **punt**. There is no kicking for conversion points or for field goals. In the realm of the kickoff there are only two types. One is for distance and possibly out of bounds near the opponents goal and the other is for the Onside kick.

A **punt** is a type of kick where the receiver catches the ball and then steps forward as he drops the ball and kicks it before it touches the ground. This type of kick is normally used on a fourth down when the team has long yardage to make and is on their own side of the midfield line. It is intended to move the ball as far away from the teams own goal line as possible.

The team receiving the punt must have five players on the line and the normal formation for the kicking team is all players are on the line with only the punter behind the line. The receiving team cannot rush the punter. Neither team can charge the other team until the ball has been kicked. On both kickoffs and punts, the kicking team may recover a kicked ball but may not advance the ball.

Proper Blocking Stance.

According to the rules put down in Chapter 6, you are given a definition of the blocking technique which is as follows.

The offense may contact opponents with their arms provided: The elbows are entirely outside the shoulders. The hands are closed or cupped with the palms not facing the opponent. The forearms are approximately parallel to the ground, in the same horizontal plane and extended not more than 45 degrees from the body.

The blocker's hands may not be locked nor may the blocker throw, or flip his elbow or forearm so that it is moving faster than his shoulders at the time of contact. The block must be between the waist and the shoulder of the opponent with at least one foot in contact with the ground at the time of the block.

The stance is best done with players using a knee flexed posture, with the body balanced evenly on both balls of the feet set at least shoulder width apart. The balanced flex knee position applies to every sport. Boxing, tennis, baseball, basketball, hockey, karate and soccer begins every action move from this fundamental position.

The only player on the team which will have his head down at the start of the play is the center. He is the closest to taking the knuckle down line position. The reason we avoid this position is to avoid any possibility of a neck injury. At this youth level of play we are not power blocking the opponent.

Blocking at the Line.

The intention of the offensive lineman is primarily to prevent the opponent from getting into the backfield to break up the play. Mostly he wants to contain and restrain his opponents movements. He does this by shoving against his opponent with his forearms. He must also be able to move latterly to prevent the defensive player from getting past him.

In the event he has been assigned the job of being a designated receiver, he must engage and move his opponent out of the way in order to get open for the pass. This effectively nullifies his opponent from reaching the backfield and allows him to be open for a brief moment. "At the line assignments" will vary depending on the play pattern called for by the QB.

Blocking on the Run.

This is also a most important function of the linemen. If a running play is the "action" play, his job is to run <u>interference</u> for the ball carrier and block any opponent in his way to protect the ball carrier. He will know prior to the snap which direction the play is going and set himself to do two things. Initially he must contain the opponent directly across from himself, then move in the direction of the play and interfere with any opponent he comes in contact with.

In sweep plays around the end, all linemen on that side of the center move in unison leading the ball carrier around that side. What is normally done is to load one side of the offensive line with both wide receivers and the QB will carry. That does not mean you can't put a man in motion and have the QB also block for the ball carrier.

Blocking by the Backfield.

All three players which constitute the backfield must understand how to block. That's both **running backs** and the **quarterback.** In a number of plays they protect each other while putting a play into action. This is done during a hand-off, pitch-out and flare passes. It is also done when the **running backs** will run interference for the **quarterback** on a sweep play.

Quite often it is used when you are sending the **tackles** out as **tight ends** of a play. The receivers have their own play patterns which require blocking in the backfield to give them time to get into position for a reception. Again it comes in handy when any lineman is assigned the receiving job. Such as short yardage by the **center.**

Defense

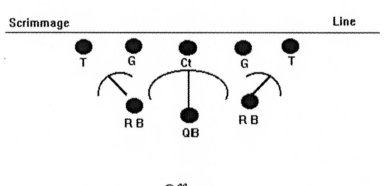

Offense

The Passing Tree.

This "Tree" is coined from NFL passing plays and routes run by the intended receivers. Some, but not all of the routes are deemed as spot passes wherein the receiver must get to a spot on the field in order to catch the pass. Many passes will be to an area where the receiver is catching on the run. The receivers route is predetermined.

In Flag Football, everyone is an eligible receiver. That means all members of the team must have an opportunity to experience each type of passing play on the tree. Short out's and short in's are the pass staples for the **Category I** (3/4 grade) player. As we develop our plays later, the team will better understand how it works.

An example might be that both Wide Receivers go out from each end of the line. The left side may go short down and in while the other goes short down and out.

Running Patterns for the Pass Play

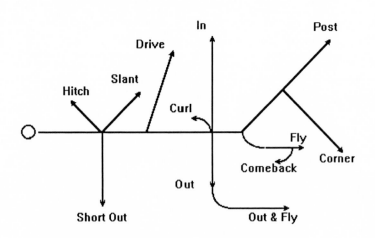

This is referred to as the "Passing Tree".

Passing Pattern for Offensive Middle Linemen.

The Center and both Guards are normally used for the short yardage gains. At the snap of the ball, the designated lineman receiver goes straight out, then posts up to receive the pass. Which ever of the linemen that flanked the intended receiver, must work together to close the gap created by the receiving lineman's rushing forward for the pass reception..

This is a quick play, and used when short yardage must be gained and often used to pick up the conversion points. According to the rules, One point conversion: The ball shall be placed on the 2 yard line for the attempt. Two point conversion: The ball shall be placed on the 5 yard line.

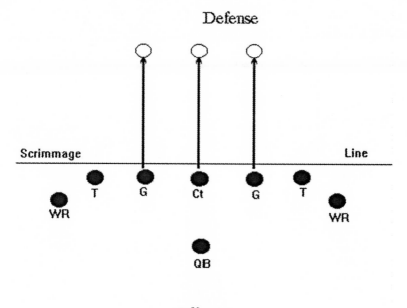

Passing Pattern for Offensive Tackles.

Both Tackles are eligible receivers and are often involved in going out with the **Wide Receiver** for a double reception opportunity. Let's say that the WR on the right side is going straight out on a fly and the left Tackle is down and in. Now the QB has two options available for him to choose from, not excluding a forced run.

Regardless of the choice the QB makes, the receiver now has a blocker near enough to help him gain yardage. The point we are making is that the **Tackle** is used to pick up greater yardage than the **Center** or the **Guards**. That does not mean that they are not used for short yardage gains. Like the other linemen, **Tackles** may also be used in getting the conversion points.

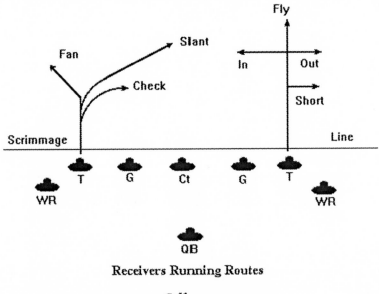

Receivers Running Routes

Offense

You should view the **tackles** as being like a **tight end** in regulation football. He's and eligible receiver and also a blocker. Therefore when you put two **wide receivers** on one side of the line, the **tackle** will do what a **tight end** would do.

Passing Pattern for Offensive Running Backs.

In flag football, when the **wide receivers** pull back several steps behind the line, they assume the formation features of running backs. Because running backs begin their pass routes from several steps behind the line of scrimmage, their choice of pass patterns differs slightly from those of wide receivers who are closer to the offensive line.

There are a variety of plays in which this formation will be called for. It will apply for both running and passing plays, hand-offs, laterals and flare passes which are returned to the QB for a pass downfield. It is valuable in creating deception of the intended play and throwing the defense off guard.

During practice and real games, the offensive formation may change in many ways. We will create strong side/weak side formations for sweeps and passes.

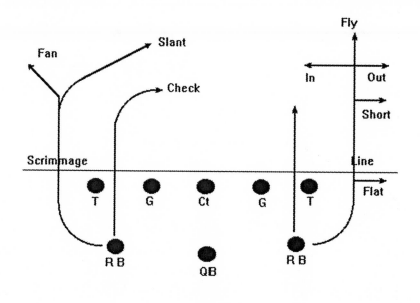

Offense

Passing Pattern for Offensive Wide Receivers.

The **wide receivers** run all of the pass routes shown in the passing tree diagram. And those are only a partial design of the many routes that are available. In a game, these basics are expanded upon to reflect the body moves of the receiver to deceive the defensive secondary. At the level of 3/4 grades we have reduced our routes of receiver running patterns to accommodate the children's abilities.

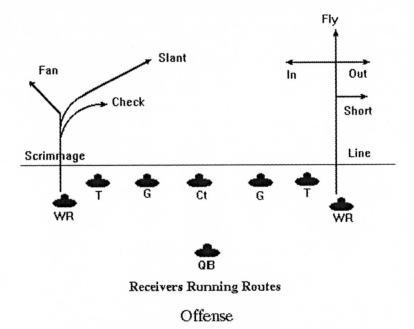

Receivers Running Routes

Offense

All receivers run patterns or routes to break free from the defenders and get open for the play. There are different distances for every route during the play, and this distance will vary with the ability of the QB to make the pass. You will have to teach your players to run for the ball, get under it. This is known as spot passing or passing to a pre designated target area. They can't expect to hit the assigned mark and stop to receive the pass. However that is what they usually do.

Putting a Man in Motion.

Putting a man in motion creates a number of advantages for the offense. First it creates an **unbalanced line** with a weak side and a strong side situation. This allows offense to have additional blocking in the event it is a running play around the strong side or additional receivers for a passing play. Defense must counter the move as quickly as possible before the snap. It's up to the middle linebacker to call for the defensive shift.

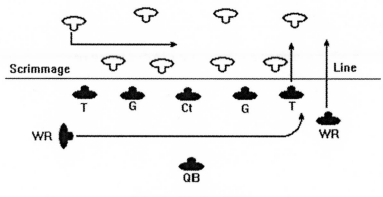

Man in Motion Play

The man in motion can reach his position behind the line as the ball is snapped and be prepared to receive a lateral pass for a run around the end, or to make a pass across the field to a **tackle** that has gone downfield, or a pass back to the **QB** who may then pass to a **receiver** that has gone downfield.

The man in motion may also receive a hand-off if the snap is made as he is going into motion from his behind line position. Defense then must adjust as to does he have it? Or is it a fake hand-off and the QB is going to pass or run the ball. In flag football, the defense normally makes an adjustment in the secondary to cover or back up the unbalanced line.

Motion can be very effective against defense which is using a man-to-man coverage. The objective of the man in motion may be to create a weak spot in the defense leaving an area open where the defender has made his shift from. It is always the weathervane for what defense has set itself to do.

In summary, putting a man in motion sets the stage for a variety of potential plays. It puts a receiver in position behind the offensive line to be a lead blocker for a running play around the end he has shifted to. It can bring a receiver into the backfield in time to make him a potential ball carrier on an around the end sweeps or for a reverse play. It places a running back closer to the outside prior to execution of a play, in a position where he can take a quick pitchout or flare pass, or can become a lead blocker. It also helps flood that side of the line with potential pass receivers.

The Shotgun.

The QB lines up four or five yards behind the center and away from the possible "blitz" conditions just behind the center. Instead of having to take several backward steps to be in passing position, he is already in the position to read the defense. It gives the QB perhaps a second or a second and a half more time to find his open receivers and avoid the defensive rush.

It does not preclude a running play such as a hand-off or a reverse from a man in motion, it primarily gives the QB more time in the execution of the play. If there is a downside to the formation, it would be the **center** having to make an upside down pass to the **QB**. The **center** must also move quickly after the snap to play the offensive line position or break forward in some cases for a pass.

In the typical shotgun play, the **QB** is isolated and the **receivers** are spread. In the event one side has been flooded with **receivers,** the **QB** will move in that direction after the snap in order to make his passing play. Now there exists two options; a sweeping run around the end that is flooded or to pass to an intended receiver.

The Running Routes.

In Flag Football the primary restriction for the running routes is that you cannot run through the center of the line of scrimmage. A marker is placed on each side of the football prior to the snap, defining the zone through which the ball carrier cannot run. Markers are spaced at 2 1/2 yards on either side of the ball. Penalty for running through the middle will be automatic dead ball, at the line of scrimmage and loss of down.

The running backs, including the **QB** may run through the line at any point open and available to them. The man in motion may go from one side of the line to the other, and if given the ball, cut through the line or run a sweep. Each running back when in the possession of the ball may advance the ball forward through any route shown below. If a reverse is run, the ball carrier remains restricted from running through the center of the line.

Defense

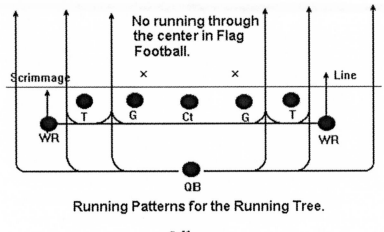

No running through the center in Flag Football.

Running Patterns for the Running Tree.

Offense

This restriction of running the ball through the center of the line should not be confused with passing over and through the center of the line by the QB in a passing play. The passing over the center to a receiver in position is the standard "dump" pass used for short yardage gains during play.

The 3-4 Defense.

In Flag Football, we set up in a different way than in regulation football because the running backs cannot run through the center of the scrimmage line. We set a defensive guard directly ahead of the center in the same position a nose tackle would take. The other defensive guard and a defensive end set up directly across from the offensive line tackles and slightly towards the center near the guards.

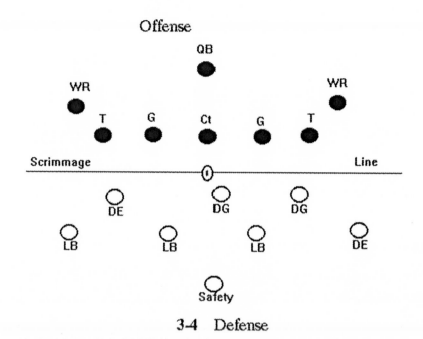

3-4 Defense

Behind the front three, we place the three linebackers with the other end playing towards the outside. Directly behind the second line of four players is the Cornerback or safety. Everything behind the front line is considered as the secondary in this formation. Defense must decide as quickly as possible whether it's a running play or a pass play.

Usually the offensive line will charge the defense if the play is a running play, and conversely, hold ground if it's a passing play. If it's a running play the defensive ends must rush in to contain the runner, and the man playing the nose tackles position tries to punch through the line and break up the play. The linebackers move in the direction of the flow to close down a sweep around the end. The safety becomes a backup to the line backers when the ball carrier has passed the line of scrimmage.

The linebackers also have pass coverage responsibilities that will vary with each play. They are responsible for covering any offensive lineman that breaks into the backfield as a potential pass receiver. It is also their job to pick up and cover wide receivers who are breaking down the sidelines. The safety must cover the receiver who is running the fly pattern from his position behind the linemen in the secondary.

When the offense floods one side to create the strong side/weak side situation, the linebackers shift to cover the rush from the wide or chosen receivers. This begins when the man-in-motion begins his move towards an already weighted side.

The 4-3 Defense.

The gained advantage of the four men on the line, is that they can better put pressure on the backfield. Where in the 3-4 defense, a defensive lineman can be double teamed by an offensive guard and offensive tackle. Penetration of the down linesmen is now easier since it can become a man-to-man offense/defense situation. The defense now has a better chance of rushing the QB and getting a sack or breaking up a play.

The defensive ends are also in an improved position to prevent a run around the end and can force the play back towards the middle. In this type of football, this formation has proven very effective. As a matter of fact, the NFL still exploits it a lot With slight modification it becomes the ideal platform for the blitz. In the blitz situation, the philosophy calls for the rush to the backfield over the defense of an intended pass receiver.

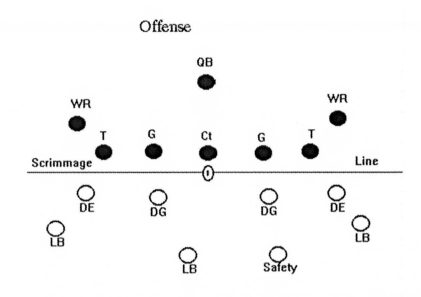

4-3 Defense

In the 3-4 defensive situation, we have pressure on the receiver. In the 4-3 defense, we put pressure on the pass origin. The resulting effect for the linebackers is that they must now cover more territory than in the 3-4 assignment. Another thing that is gained by having the extra lineman is the improved ability to stop a run through the line. In almost all cases, the defensive linemen are expected to rush the ball carrier in the backfield, get penetration.

Now this is not always true. The middle linebacker may read the offense and call for what is termed the FLEX. That is when defense goes from "act upon" to the "react to", mode. This is when the defense will read the play, then react to it. It is used primarily to shut down the running play through the line. If the middle linebacker calls the signal for the FLEX the linebackers shift closer to the line.

Basically, it's stop the offensive running backs at the line. With seven men close to the line of scrimmage, it's doubtful the offense will get far when trying to run through the line. The middle linebacker is the counterpart to the offensive quarterback. He may call an audible at the line to change the defensive game plan.

The defensive coordinator may flash a signal to the middle linebacker indicating which defensive formation he feels will best work based upon his observation or anticipation of what the offensive is going to do. It can be three finger raised for the 3-4 formation or four fingers for the 4-3 formation. He can call a blitz with a raised clinched first which the middle linebacker then passes to the defensive unit.

The 3-3-2 Defense.

This defensive formation is best used when the offensive line has been spread and a long pass downfield is anticipated. It places two safeties or cornerbacks in the backfield to pick up the receivers who are now running a "fly" pass route or pattern.

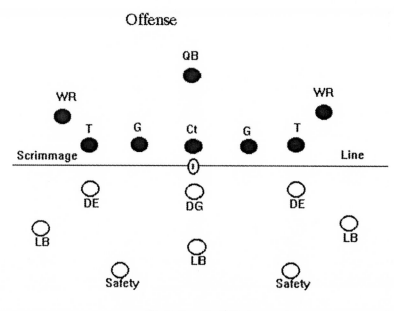

Offense

3-3-2 Defense

The first to pick up the receiver would be the outside linebacker as the receiver comes over the line of scrimmage. The safety then moves in to add pressure on the receiver and the quarterback who is going to go for the long pass. This is most often used in the third down, long yardage situation where the team in possession of the ball must give it their best effort.

This is not without it's flaws. It can open the door for the QB to run with the ball and gain yardage. It may allow the offensive formation to shift to a strong side/weak side formation, and generate a run around the end. So in this formation, the down linesmen must rush the backfield to put pressure on the QB. In the line up of linebackers, the middle linebacker will shift towards the strong side, and the strong side line backer moves slightly further out.

In the defensive secondary, the safeties will shift towards the strong side of the formation, with the weak side safety remaining close to the center of the formation. He remains aware of the possibility of a gadget play coming his way since defense has shifted to the strong side.

The Zones Defense.

All players who are not down linesmen are active in a pre-assigned zone which they must cover. The defensive backfield must stay alert to where the intended receivers are going and converge on the player when the ball is thrown. The defensive back nearest the intended receiver will anticipate the pass and close on the receiver to either break up the play with a deflection or attempt to intercept the ball.

There are two areas in the zone. One is the near zone closest to the line, the other is further back extending to the goal line. This is where the cornerback or safety is responsible for coverage. The deep zone coverage cannot allow the intended receiver to get behind him and open for the play.

In Flag Football, almost every linebacker and backfield back have a double zone assignment. That is they must cover close behind the line and deep behind the line for passing plays. If the ball is not thrown by the time the ball carrier crosses the line of scrimmage, all defensive backs converge towards the ball carrier.

The reason the defensive backfield maintains a zone defense is to make sure that a hand-off which may appear to be a running play is not converted to a passing play by the offensive running back with the ball. It is done a lot in this game, and done effectively. We will cover more on that later in the book when we begin designing pass action and running plays for the offense.

In summary, zone assignments are intended to cover pass action plays by putting coverage where the intended receiver will be heading. It is geared primarily for that, but it will also cover the break away run that a good back may generate with excellent blocking from his team at the line.

Offense

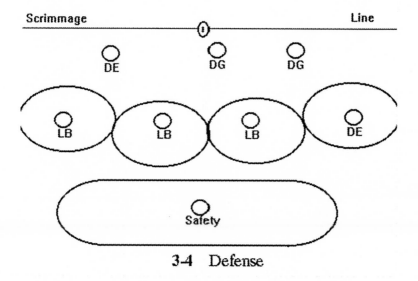

3-4 Defense

This illustration of the 3-4 Defense gives a simple display of what we have been discussing.

The Man-to-Man Defense.

The offense in this case may have the advantage when the intended receiver has single man coverage. Single man coverage on a receiver is hard to learn and to execute. In man-to-man the linebackers must cover the running backs or linemen who come out of the backfield or off the line for a pass play.

The cornerbacks and safeties must pick up the wide receivers as they break downfield. Their job is to keep the receiver between the quarterback and themselves. Backpedaling off their position, they must mirror every move the wide receiver makes until the ball is thrown, and then move in to deflect the ball or intercept. Timing is everything in this situation.

The biggest drawback of man-to-man coverage is that it is basically a personnel match up that sometimes turns into a footrace to the ball. When you have only one defender between the goal line and the offense's best wide receiver, one defensive misstep could mean six points for the other team. Easy to see, tall and fast against short and quick. Tall will get it every time.

The Bump and Run.

In the typical bum and run situation, a defensive back will position himself directly across from the wide receiver. As the ball is snapped and the wide receiver comes across the line of scrimmage, the defensive back moves in to make contact or bump the wide receiver. The defensive back can only make contact within the first five yards of the line, beyond that it is considered illegal contact.

After the initial bump, the defensive back will trail right behind the wide receiver as he runs his route. The defensive back must concentrate on every move the receiver makes. He cannot worry about when the pass is thrown, he does not look back for the ball until the receiver does. The back must not take an inside fake or the receiver will run right past him. He can take an outside fake, allowing the receiver to run towards the middle where he has help waiting.

What the defensive back is trying to accomplish in the bump and run is to break up the pass play. He stalls the wide receiver in making a fast break to the backfield and may have a chance for an interception in case the ball is poorly thrown. In Flag Football, any lineman coming of the line heading for the backfield should be bumped or stalled and the secondary will pick him up.

At The Goal Defense.

This is always a tough situation for defense. At this point, they are the blockers containing the offensive line and if possible punching inside to break up the quarterback's play. All defensive players with the exception of two safeties or a linebacker and a safety/cornerback is on the line. The modified secondary must be quick to evaluate the play action and react accordingly.

Offense

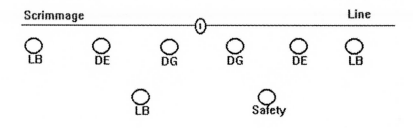

Short Yardage - Goal Line Defense

The secondary can anticipate a "dump" pass to the center who jumps across the line or a pass into the end zone at the outsides. If the conversion is set for a two point conversion, it's a sure bet to be a pass action play, the only question is where. As a consequence, the down linesmen must bump their opponents and get into the backfield as quickly as possible.

Sweep runs may also be the offensive option from a strong side where a reverse is also possible. The preceding illustration offers a strong defense against the running play and would be called for by the defensive coordinator or the middle linebacker once defense can read the offensive play. Whatever the case, this would be the initial lineup of the defensive unit on the field.

The option to the defensive formation which offers better pass protection is below.

Offense

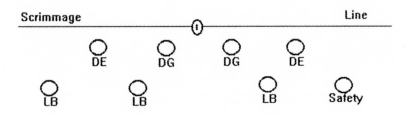

Short Yardage - Goal Line Defense

As shown, the secondary is just behind the down linesmen and ready to pick up an intended pass receiver coming through the line. The secondary will shift three of the four defensive backs towards the strong side, in a strong side situation. The weak side safety will remain in his current position to thwart a reverse pass play in his zone.

Dogs & Blitzes Defense.

The purpose of the pass rush is to increase the pressure primarily on the QB and either foil the passing attempt or to sack the quarterback. To maximize this effort, the defense will occasionally rush extra men from unexpected positions.

Dog: A linebacker or any combination of linebackers will leave their regular area of coverage and streak past the line of scrimmage at the snap of the ball. Their job is to break into the backfield through any available holes in the offensive line. The primary objective is to break up the passing play and sack the quarterback. This is a surprise move by defense.

Blitz: Involves the secondary coming in from the sides, alone or in combination with linebackers to shut down the play. It closes off the quarterback sneak and option play. It is clearly intended to sack the quarterback, but it leaves intended pass receivers open. Again, this is a surprise rush play and may be feinted to throw the quarterback off of his intended pass play.

When a defensive player either dogs or blitzes, he has the element of surprise in his favor. Therefore the defensive player must disguise his intentions prior to the snap. The defensive player does this by not moving too quickly, not committing to soon.

Force Defense.

There are certain areas of the field which must be defended at all costs. The most crucial of these is the outside on a running play. The outside linebacker or safety must not let the ball carrier get outside him, because he could be the last defender between the ball carrier and the goal line. He must force the runner towards the middle where he may pick up help or make the play by himself.

SPECIAL TEAMS.

Special teams are for kickoffs, kickoff returns, Onside kicks, punting and punt returns in Flag Football. It's not as complex as the formations found in regulation football in high school, college or the NFL but they do have their place. And youngsters like being on "special teams."

Kickoffs.

Let's review the rules for kickoffs and kickoff returns which from the rules section earlier in this book.

On kickoffs. the kicking team may use any formation as long as the entire team is behind their restraining line and in bounds. The receiving team may use any formation as long as the entire team is behind their restraining line and at least 3 players are within five yards of the restraining line.

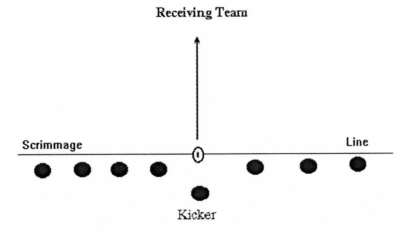

Members of the kicking team are divided and spread across the field behind the restraining line. The kicker is in the middle of the line and each man has an assignment to follow the ball downfield while remaining in their respective lane routes. The men in the middle of the formation must have aggressive pursuit skills and the outside members must possess good speed.

The men in the middle are required to break through the receivers wedge formation which the ball carrier will try to use in order to gain ground behind a blocking front. The outside members of the kicking team must be able to sprint down and drive the ball carrier towards the middle or to strip his flags on an end run. The kicker usually hangs back to act as a safety in the event the ball carrier gets free and must be run down by the kicker.

Flexibility in the pursuit is a must. The kicker, if he decides to kick to one side or the other, must inform his formation of his intention prior to the kick. He may do that to avoid kicking to a very good return man and take a chance on a less capable ball carrier. With all members of the kicking team aware of this intention, they will converge towards the anticipated receiver.

Squib Kicks.

Squib kicks are a low, line drive type of kick which hits the ground and bounces crazily in almost any direction. It avoids getting the ball to a dangerous return man and makes it difficult for the receiving team to recover. This sometimes happens by accident, but normally it is by design, and again, if a squib kick is going to be made, the kicking formation will be informed prior to the attempt.

Kickoff Returns.

The receiving team may use any formation as long as the entire team is behind their restraining line and at least 3 players are within five yards of the restraining line. The midfield line shall act as the restraining line for the receiving team.

At the restraining line, the linesmen should be five line blockers, who will form a blocking front line to slow or severely impede the rush of the kicking teams players. One of the lines first order of business is to guard against a possible Onside kick. Once the ball is kicked, the linesmen may form a wedge in the center of the field or shift the wedge towards either side to help the kick returner to gain ground.

The front line should consist of quick offensive or defensive linemen, or linebackers who block well and have good hands for receiving in the event we have an Onside kick or a poorly kicked ball. The men in the backfield are normally spread with the center man slightly further back than the other two.

The backfield should consist of wide receivers, running backs or defensive backs who are used to handling the ball. The prerequisites for the backfield assignments are good hands, speed and ability to read the defensive rush coming towards them. When the ball is received by anyone of the three men in the backfield, the other two will run blocking interference for the ball carrier.

Receiving Formation

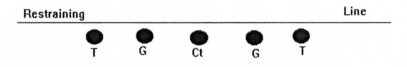

Onside Kicks.

The Onside kick is most frequently used late in the game by the team that is behind in score, needing one more possession for a scoring opportunity, and is racing the clock. Usually the receiving team in most cases will recover the ball, therefore it isn't used in the early part of the game. If used early, it can give the receiving team a decided advantage near mid field and better field position than they might have in a regular kickoff.

The kickoff becomes a free ball once it has traveled at least 10 yards and can be recovered by either team. *On both kickoffs and punts, the kicking team may recover a kick but may not advance the ball.* This is how it is played. The Onside kick rule takes advantage of this, and the kicking teams objective is to recover the ball before the receiving team can get to it.

In the execution of the Onside kick, the kicking team must have good quick players on the line who possess good hands for recovering the ball. Now the ball may be kicked with a soft low arcing flight or it may be driven like a squib kick, bounding and jumping along its path. The kicker tries to aim at a predetermined area, 10 yards or more away so the kicking team can make a legal recovery.

The effort when made often tries to use deception and hide the idea of an Onside kick from the receiving team, however if it's late in the game the coach may call for an overload shift to the side he intends to kick too. He calls for the overload just prior to the kick. This is considered a desperate effort by the kicking team but it can work because of the additional men making the recovery effort.

Recovering Onside Kicks.

If late in the game, the receiving team suspects an attempted Onside kick is coming, it will insert it's own special team to recover the ball.

Like the kicking team, the receiving team must have good quick players on the line who possess good hands for recovering the ball. Such as tight ends, wide receivers, running backs, and defensive backs. All of the players should be accustomed to handling the ball.

One thing that can happen, is the kicking team will see the Onside recovery formation and kick a long kickoff. This tends to scramble the recovery teams ability to make a lengthy return down field. Anything can happen to change these plans. It could be both teams have aligned themselves on one side of the field with the lone receiver far downfield and the kicker kicks the ball in the opposite direction and follows it for a recovery.

Punt Coverage

On both kickoffs and punts, the kicking team may recover a kick but may not advance the ball. The fair catch rule can be invoked.

In Flag Football, there is no rushing the punter to block the kick. Instead the punting team aligns itself behind the line of scrimmage and waits for the kick to be made after the ball is snapped. Once the ball is kicked, the team may rush forward and attempt a recovery if possible and if not possible, strip the flags from the punt receiver.

The punting team should be made up of tight ends, wide receivers, running backs, and defensive backs. All of these players should be accustomed to handling the ball. Their aggressive skills and quickness are a decided advantage in getting downfield after the ball. The kicker will remain near the line after the kick to act as a safety in the event the punt returner breaks free and is headed for a goal.

Like the kickoff team, the punting team has routes to run in order to have adequate coverage across the field. The outside linesmen are responsible for forcing the return man towards the middle of the field where there is help waiting.

The kicker, if he decides to kick to one side or the other, must inform his formation of his intention prior to the kick. He may do that to avoid kicking to a very good return man and take a chance on a less capable ball carrier. With all members of the kicking team aware of this intention, they will converge towards the anticipated receiver.

Punt Returns.

On punts, the receiving team must have five players on the line of scrimmage.

The receiving team should be the normal offensive team with the offensive linemen in place at the restraining line. The linesmen should be prepared to block the man directly ahead of him to impede that players line of pursuit. This is the case of man-to-man coverage at the line where it will do the most good. The receiving team knows that the kicking team has routes to run and must take advantage of that.

The backfield should consist of wide receivers, running backs or defensive backs who are used to handling the ball. The prerequisites for the backfield assignments are good hands, speed and ability to read the defensive rush coming towards them. When the ball is received by anyone of the three men in the backfield, the other two will run blocking interference for the ball carrier.

When the punt is in the air, the returner must concentrate totally on the flight of the ball and ignore the onrushing defense. He can make one of two choices. Either call for a fair catch by waving his arms while the ball is still in flight, or catch the ball and make his run for it. He cannot avoid taking the ball because the ball is considered a live ball and can be recovered by the punting team. He cannot have his flags pulled before he receives the ball.

It may appear that the running backs or punt returnee's have no plan of action at all, but that is not true. The receiving team may use force to move downfield along one side or the other, or to go straight down the center. This is determined in the huddle prior to the punt being made and controlled by the special teams coach.

Chapter 9

Flag Football Offense

The Shotgun.

The **QB** lines up three or four yards behind the line and away from the possible "blitz" conditions just behind the **center**. Instead of having to take several backward steps to be in passing position, he is already in the passing position and able to read the defense. It gives the QB perhaps a second or a second and a half more time to put his play action into operation and avoid the defensive rush.

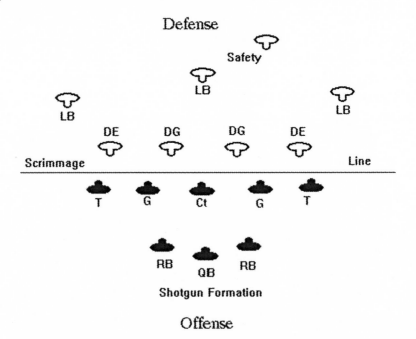

Shotgun Formation

In the typical shotgun play, the **QB** is flanked by the running backs who have positions on either side and slightly forward of the **QB's** position. Prior to the snap of the ball, the **QB** may have optioned to run either to the right or left side of the line for a sweeping run. This would have been decided in the huddle.

The job of the **down linesmen** is to contain the defense and provide block coverage for the direction of the sweep. The **running backs** have the responsibility for blocking on the run for the QB around that end of the line which was pre-selected.

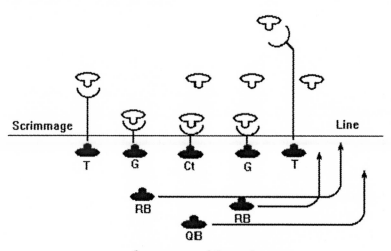

Sweep around the end zone.

This is the basic running play by the **QB**, provided he has the speed and agility to pull it off. However it is not the only running play from the backfield. Either of the **running backs** may also become the ball carrier during a sweep around the end. When we use a running back as the ball carrier, the **QB** runs blocking interference.

At the snap of the ball for instance, the left side **running back** may cross in front of the QB for a hand-off to run the sweep. Or the QB may fake a hand-off to the **left back** and hand it to the **right back** as the play unfolds. What the action calls for is a deception to confuse defense as to who is the ball carrier.

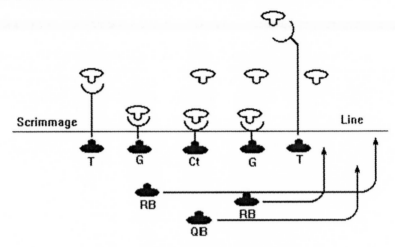

Hand off to the RB for a right hand sweep.

So far we are speaking only of running plays from the shotgun position, but we also use it for a reverse direction passing play. In Flag Football, you can pass more than once from behind the line, it is usually limited to two passes behind the line of scrimmage.

As an example, the right side **running back** would run to his right as the ball is snapped and the left **running back** would run to his left, the **QB** would throw or pitch a short pass to the right side **running back** then break to his left, following the left side **running back**. The ball carrier would then stop, turn in the direction taken by the left **running back** and the **QB**.

He now has two options, Pass to the **QB** or the other **running back** for a sweep around the far end. If the **QB** receives the ball, he has two options, run or make a passing play down field. The choice will be the coaches call.

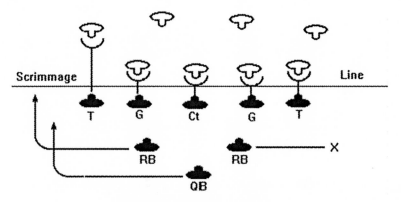

Behind the line flare pass off.

The behind the line passing opens the door to a wide number of plays which can be generated using this rule in Flag Football. It's up to you to expand the potential available, and that's almost limitless.

The intention of showing these illustrations is to lay the ground work for your expansion upon these most basic of plays. It's great fun to design an action play and have it actually be a success. You're going to do that anyway, it is human nature to lay order to what is otherwise chaos and that is what you are involved with.

Also note that the center may snap the ball to either of the running backs instead of to the quarterback.

The Spread.

Again the **QB** lines up three or four yards behind the line and away from the possible "blitz" conditions just behind the **center**. It gives the QB perhaps a second or a second and a half more time to find his open receivers and avoid the defensive rush. As you notice, the **running backs** are shifted forward to a position just back of the line by approximately two yards and become **wide receivers**.

This formation provides the greatest amount of protection to the QB when the play action begins. You have a seven man offensive line as compared to a four or five man defensive line. It's the ideal formation for the pass action play. It also offers the advantage of having your receivers closer to the line from which their speed will give them added penetration into the defensive backfield.

This diagram is an example of the routes to be run by the intended receivers on a pass action play. We have put both wide receivers into action along with a tackle serving as a tight end.

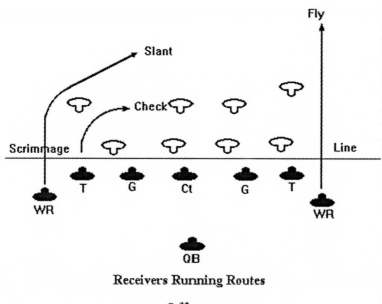

Receivers Running Routes

Offense

The first consideration by the **QB** is to read the mismatch by the defense against one of the potential receivers. By that, I mean by physical size. If the **receiver** is decidedly taller than his opponent, go for him and avoid an interception.

If you recall the "passing tree" from chapter 8, the receivers routes may fit any variety of choices. That again will be decided by you and your team as to what works best for you. If you have a very young team, pass routes may be shortened, or if you have an older team of boys, they may be enlarged.

We also put a man-in-motion for a hand-off and a run around the end. We can also get the man-in-motion plays going, with hand-offs and behind the line passes. Generate sweeps around one end or the other and in general make a large number of quickly executed play.

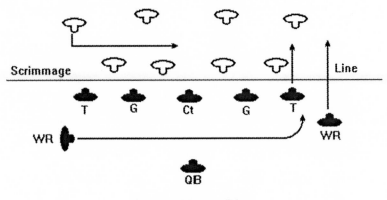

Man in Motion Play

In this example we execute the simple hand-off to sweep around the right end. The **defensive back** will cover the man-in-motion by crossing behind his line to stay up with the ball carrier. It becomes the **right tackle** and **right receivers** job to set up the offensive blocking run. The **QB** will run the back-door on the play to prevent defense from catching the ball carrier from behind.

So far we have shown the basic spread pattern as having flexibility to be either a pass action or a running play, both from the same basic formation. We also use it as a "gadget play", where we create an unexpected change of play to confuse the defense.

As an example, we begin the play action with a man-in-motion as if we were running a sweep around the end. This pulls the defensive back along with the moving receiver in the direction the receiver is moving behind the line of scrimmage. What we are accomplishing with this is to weaken the defense on the left side of the line.

After the hand-off is made the **QB** moves towards the left as the left **tackle** drives downfield on a fly route. The ball carrier stops behind the line instead of making a sweep around the end and passes back to the

QB who then has two options. If the **tackle** is well covered he will run around left end, and if the **tackle** is open, pass to the **tackle** downfield.

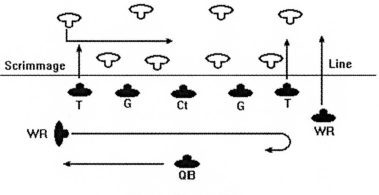

Man in Motion Play

These plays are the most fundamental which can be generated by the basic formation. Again, it's up to you to expand on what is offered and make more actions plays which are uniquely your own and belong to you and your team. You might even make some simple sketches to give to your boys and allow them to design a play or two.

The Slot.

Again the QB lines up three or four yards behind the line and away from the possible "blitz" conditions just behind the **center.** What we have done is to place both **backs** as **wide receivers** on one end of the offensive line. It doesn't matter which side, the right or the left, it is still the slot formation.

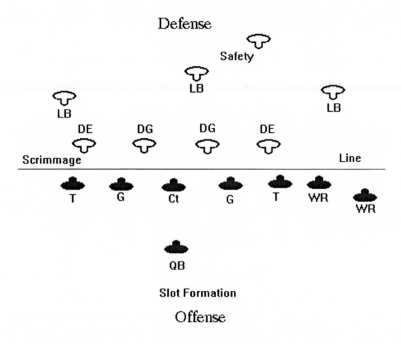

Slot Formation

Offense

This basic formation is used a lot because the running routes of the receivers can become so varied. We have in effect overloaded one side of the offensive line. Here we show it as the right hand side of the line, it can also be on the left hand side of the offensive line. We are also in the position to make the weak side **tackle** an active **receiver.**

This formation also works well for a running play by the **QB** with extra blocking coverage on the overloaded side of the line. However, as often as not we make it a pass action play.

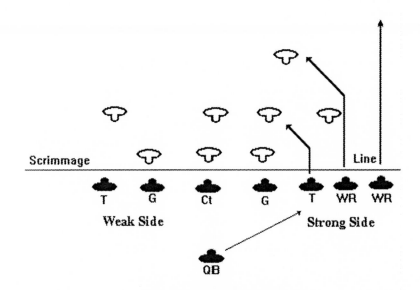

Sweep around the strong side.

On any running play, the offensive line is blocking to protect the ball carrier. In this case, the down linesmen must attempt to contain the defensive line from penetration or shifting in the direction of the ball carrier going around the end for a sweep. The right tackle and the receivers must run blocking interference against the defensive backfield which will move towards the strong side.

Overloading one side is common in Flag Football, and defense is innately aware of what must be done to cut the play to short yardage gains. However, defense doesn't always have its way, particularly if the ball carrier has enough speed to make the turn, and with a little help from blocking, break free to scramble into the end zone.

Most of the time though, it serves as a good pass play formation that has a variety of possibilities for good yardage gain. In the example below, we put both receivers and the tackle into running pass receivers routes.

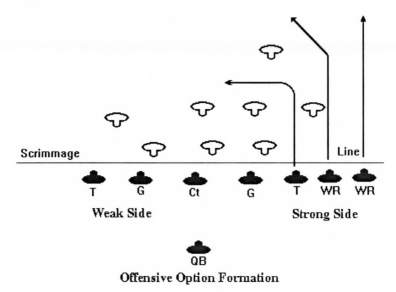

Offensive Option Formation

Smells a little of the "Pacific Coast Offense" play. Defense will set up pretty much the way you see it displayed. When an overloaded side is presented, the defensive down linesmen usually go into the 3-4 formation as you see illustrated.

We still have a simple way of expanding the offensive passing attack to include one more receiver. It is to put the weak side tackle into play as a tight end. His receiving route will be straight out on a fly pattern. The QB must make a quick read of the defense and determine which of the receivers is most open.

The offensive linemen are assigned the "hold at all costs" job, but it can't hold for long. What offense will benefit from the most is a mismatch between the speed of the intended receivers and the defenders.

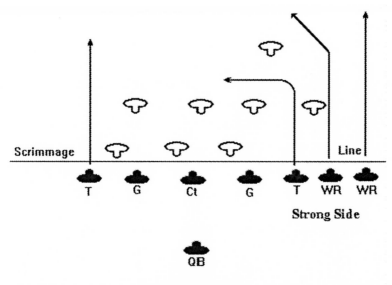

Passing Attack

A good defensive coordinator will usually tackle this problem by making sure the backfield goes for zone defense as opposed to man-to-man coverage.

So far we have illustrated a sweeping run around the end and two pass action plays. There are many more plays available from this formation than that. We could for instance pull the outside **receiver** a step or two back, make a behind the line pass to him and have him run behind the offensive line to the other end of the line.

At that point he is in position to pass to the **QB** who has begun to run his route outside with the other **receiver** and create a gadget play the defense is not ready for.

The Single Wing.

Again the QB lines up three or four yards behind the line and away from the possible "blitz" conditions just behind the **center.** What we have done is to place one of the **backs** as a **wide receiver** at one end of the offensive line. In this case we have chosen right handed as the example with the running back to the left of the QB and the **wide receiver** on the right side of the offensive line.

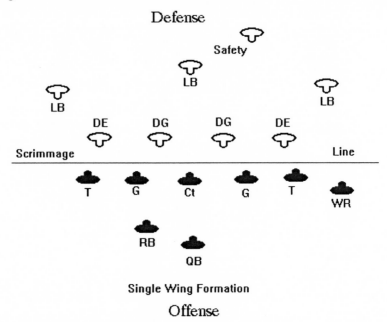

Single Wing Formation

This basic formation lends itself to a wide variety of pattern plays. With one **running back** near the QB he adds extra blocking potential and protection to the QB as a play unfolds. This formation leads into flare passes, pitch outs, and hand-offs. It has flexibility for a running or a passing play.

It easily becomes a running play with a sweep around whatever end the other **back** or **wide receiver** is on. If it were to be around the right side of the line it would look like this.

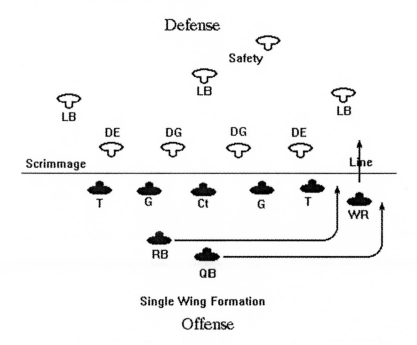

Single Wing Formation

Offense

The **tackle, running back** and **wide receiver** would run interference for the QB. Here the QB is taking the far outside route around the end zone receiving the maximum protection available by the men on the strong side of the formation.

The **offensive linemen** will move across the line of scrimmage and make the attempt to cut off the defensive linemen from moving in the direction of the ball carrier. As in all offensive plays, the offensive line is involved in controlling where possible, the defensive line from getting into position to break up the play.

This also works for the hand-off play to the **running back** who is then block covered by the **QB** as they both create an end run behind the line **wide receiver**.

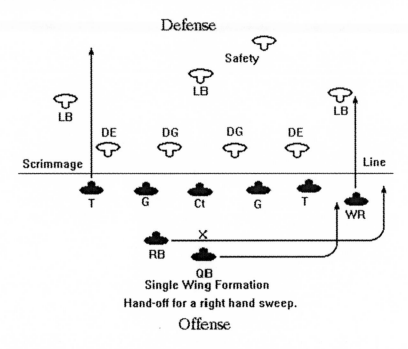

Single Wing Formation
Hand-off for a right hand sweep.

The simple hand-off to the **back** can convert to any number of possibilities for a pass action play. The **back** can stop behind the right **tackle**, and throw to any **offensive lineman** who has penetrated the defensive line. He is covered by the **wide receiver** and the **QB** who set up a blocking defense.

What is initiated as a running play is to mislead the defense and to draw the defensive backfield to the end they are expecting the run to be around. In the event the intended receiver(s) is to closely covered he can then revert to the running play.

Another example of this misdirection is when the **QB** takes the ball and moves into the right hand pocket and sets up for a pass to the left tackle who has gone out on a fly pattern and the right wide receiver is also down and on a fly.

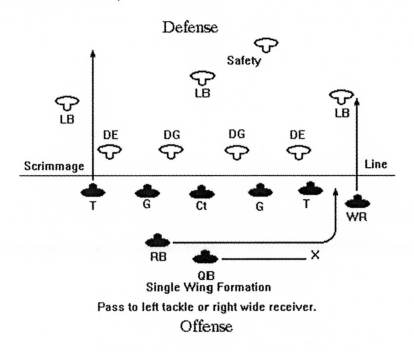

Single Wing Formation
Pass to left tackle or right wide receiver.

These are only a few simple examples of the many fundamental plays that can be generated in the single wing formation. Further misdirection may come from what appears like a sweep around the right end becomes instead, a sweep around the left end with the **running back** leading the way for the **QB**.

The I-Formation.

Has the **running backs** lined up directly behind the QB, with the QB directly behind the **center**. This is a good running formation for a running back who is able to find a line opening and get through it. It does however put a work load on the offensive linemen to force the defense aside. I don't use it, but it has potential to develop into a gadget play with hand-offs being the deception.

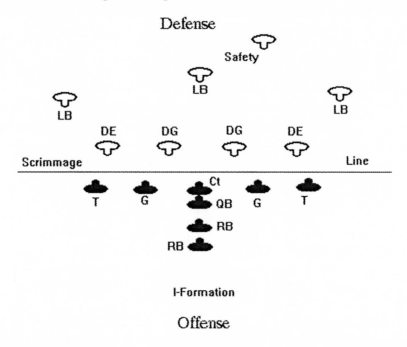

I'm trying not to be to judgmental about the formation, but with my younger teams, the line just doesn't hold well enough to give the QB protection from the **defensive guards**. The speed and dexterity of the young players is great.

If I didn't mention the famous **I-Formation**, I would feel derelict in my duties. After all, in tackle football, this formation is used over and over again. Where would the quarterback sneak be without it? Since we don't really run plays through the line behind the offensive linesmen who have created a hole in the line, we avoid it.

Goal Line Offense.

In Flag Football, the only way to get the conversion points is to either pass the ball into the end zone or to run it into the end zone. There is no kicking for the conversion points. One point conversion: The ball shall be placed on the 2 yard line for the attempt. Two point conversion: The ball shall be placed on the 5 yard line.

An example of this is using the spread formation with a wide receiver on each end of the line. Using the tackles as tight ends, they are committed to running a route as receivers. The center also dashes over the line for a possible "dump" pass.

Slant

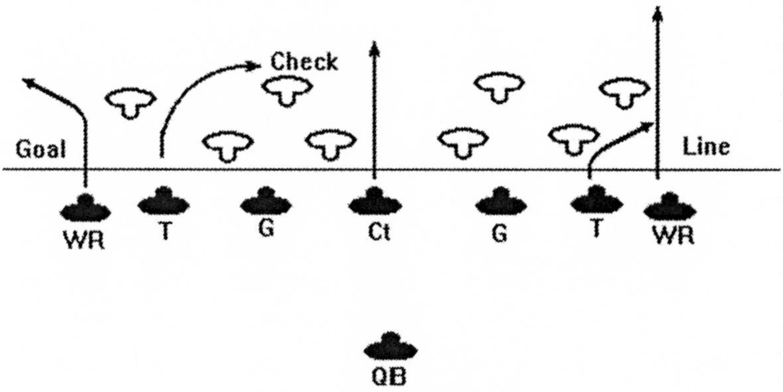

At the Goal Line Offense

Offense

In this situation the **right tackle** will head for the right corner of the end zone and the **right wide receiver** will go straight in. The **left wide receiver** will head for the left corner of the end zone and the **left tackle** will run a check route behind the line. The **center** goes straight in and posts up inside the goal line.

I have described a right handed pass action play. It also works in the left handed mode a well. All action plays can be either right or left handed as you see fit. You might also take a look at the slot, single wing and standard shotgun formation. The above play puts five men across the line. As a consequence the **QB** only has about a two second count before he either passes or runs with the ball.

Basic Formation Summary.

The basic formations we have outlined so far, form the foundation for almost all play patterns you will generate for the offensive game. They also become your basic formations to build your own plays upon. It is expected that you will expand and improve on what we have done.

Let's take for instance the Single Wing formation. That basic set up allows you to run a variety of plays. Defense reads the formation and will assume that a play you made previously from that formation will be repeated.... It won't. What you have is the flexibility of having a number of different plays from a basic formation.

That is called "generalship" of a game. You are calling the play you want run from a given formation, with a strategy to create some confusion in the defense. From most basic formations, we develop running and passing plays that add variety to the game. We also may alter the cadence of the snapping call, by that I mean the ball is moved on the first, second, or third audible from the **quarterback**.

In Chapter 8 we took the time to show the running routes for all intended receivers, we did not however extrapolate that into a diagram for each receiver to play. That will be your job! As you design your own pass action plays, lay in the route for the designated receiver to follow.

In the NFL they have play action books with hundreds of individual plays outlined. And these plays are developed from very basic formations like we have indicated here. One thing which I do with my team, is allow each boy an opportunity to design an action play. Each boy will normally submit a play that is based upon himself being the ball carrier.

Who knows? Maybe they'll give you something that you will want to use. Anyway, this gets the kids more involved with what you are trying to teach them, and it adds flavor to the team soup. Let's put the basic formations together for an overview, and something you might be able to use for your own designs.

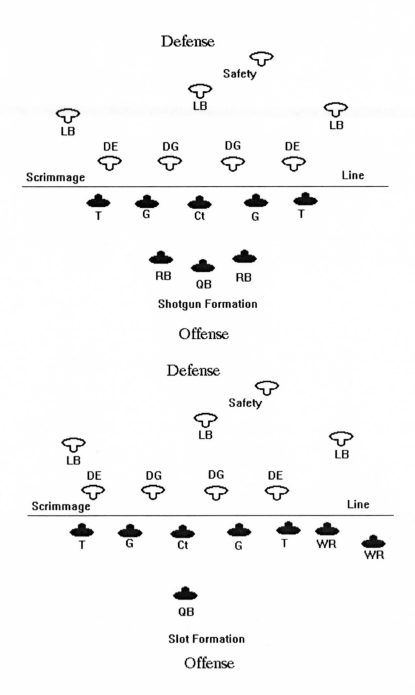

Shotgun Formation

Slot Formation

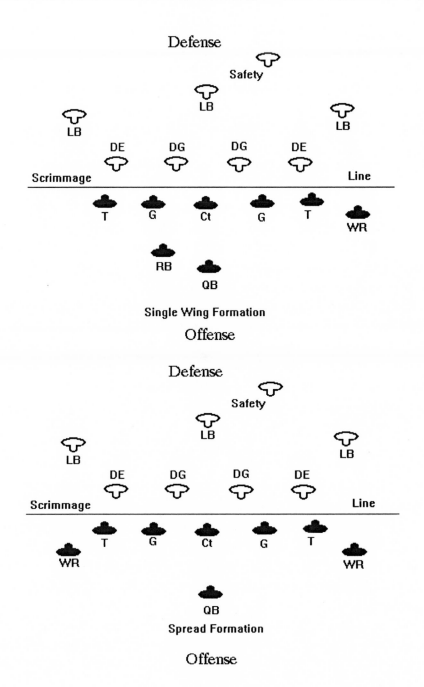

Single Wing Formation

Spread Formation

Scouting your opponent.

Yes, I do that! And more often than not, I pick up some very good training tips and ideas for myself and for my team. Other coaches have good ideas too. I will watch another team in practice as well as in a game. My first interest is to determine if that team offensively is a running team or a passing team. Secondly, is it a right handed or left handed team. By that I mean, do most of the plays go to one side or the other.

You must also evaluate the formation(s) they like to use the most and how effective they are. What formation is preferred for their pass action plays, and which is preferred for their running plays. If you will organize your list of what you are looking for prior to scouting, it becomes quite simple for gathering good data.

So far we are looking at a team for running, passing, offensive formations, and left or right handed action. What else do I need to know? Player performance. How well does the backfield perform in practice and during a game. Do the receivers have good hands? How about passing accuracy? All of this can be jotted down on a 3x5 card from your shirt pocket. Observe and record.

Seems analytical and it is. What isn't, is getting a feel for the teams moral about itself and its relationship with the coach. Do they pay attention, do they chatter while the coach is talking, do they chatter among themselves. A happy team is a tough team to beat under any circumstances, that is why good coaching techniques are so important.

You must also gather this information about any team you are playing against. What you saw in scouting may not be what you get in a game. There may have been a change or two made by the opponent. In that case, you adjust your defense based upon their offensive changes for the game.

We could be going a little far for the scope of this book, but what I wanted to pass along was the idea that there is more to the game than just going out to throw the ball around. The more detail you put into the team and the activities, the more the boys benefit.

Chapter 10

Flag Football Practice Drills

There are only six basic skills to be taught. Passing, receiving, blocking, lateral movements, running and kicking. Each skill requires instruction and practice by every member of the team. Playing a given team position brings with it a certain type of skill requirements which must be learned during drills and practices.

Basic Fundamentals

Passing the Ball.

The most important part of passing the ball is in how the ball is gripped by the throwing hand. In order to throw the spiral pass which is what we want to do, the ball is gripped at one-third of its length, with the larger portion facing the direction of the throw. Finger tips should cover the lacing and upon release, used to spin the ball.

The passing of the ball without instruction will be somewhere between an overhand pass and sidearm. What we want to do, is teach the overhand throwing method. If done properly, their accuracy will improve almost immediately, perhaps not in the vertical plane, but definitely in the horizontal.

Overhand is when the throwing arm is horizontal to the ground, the elbow bent in such a way as to place the ball almost behind the head above the shoulder. The thrower twists sideways with the free hand towards the receiver, steps forward on that foot, twists his body as he throws and ends up facing the receiver.

If the foot he steps forward on is pointing directly towards the receiver, the balls flight should be directly at the receiver. In teaching the player how to pass, we pass "to" someplace, not "at" some place. Always emphasize "to". There are four movements involved with the pass. Arm raised and cocked with player balanced. Step towards target, rotation of hips, rotation of trunk and arm extension with a wrist snap.

Receiving the Ball.

This is the hardest to teach to the young players. It isn't unusual for a boy to flinch while trying to make a reception. Players must understand that this game is played through the eyes and they must watch the ball at all times. No closing the eyes or looking away from the ball when receiving.

The ball should always be caught with both hands in order to take control of it. Because of its unusual shape, one handed catches are not very successful. They are made, but more as an exception than as a rule. There are only two conditions when a pass is received, one is on the run and the other is standing still and both must be practiced.

Passing & Receiving Drills.

Whether you form the team into two or three lines will depend on the number of players you have on your team. The starting passers will be your quarterback and alternate quarterback with the wide receivers taking over the passing chores to allow the quarterbacks to practice as receivers. The quarterback position is next to the first man in one of the lines. He will call out a run signal, sending the first player downfield for a pass.

The same happens in the other line, with a receiver going out for a pass thrown by the alternate. If the lines are ten yards apart, that will work just fine for short runs which cut to either direction. Depending on the age level of your teams players, do not extend the pass beyond twenty five yards. It's best to keep them short between five and twenty yards. As the receiver goes out, have the passer make a count of one - two - three - FIRE the ball.

The reason for the count is that during a game the line won't hold much longer than that, allowing him to make choices. That's why the QB must be able to read defense quickly and make pass/run decisions just as quickly. Alternate if possible, every player into the passing chore as you look for your best passers. Switch lines as well, allowing receivers to catch a pass from every angle.

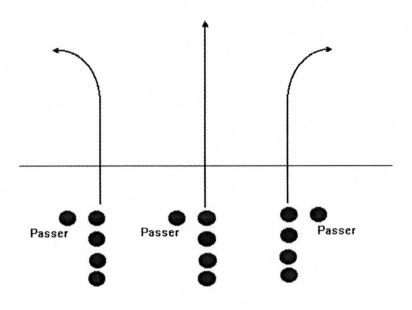

At every practice, as the boys arrive, they should start their warm-up with the passing and receiving drill. This immediately brings their focus on football. Improvements will come in leaps and bounds at each new practice or game. This is also the pre-game warm up to get them into the spirit of things. Make the running routes simple, such as down and out or down and in, or on the fly, straight out.

Progressive running routes will emerge later as we move into the pass action plays. Every member of the team should be rotated in such a way as to have him be the passer. I have never met a boy so far that did not believe he had the ability to make a passing play.

Setting Up Team Formations

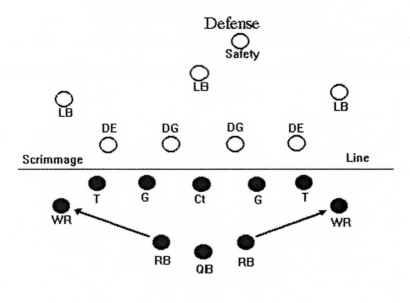

Offensive Formation.

Every member of the team should know where every position in the formation is located. When we consider the offensive formations basic structure, we show how the repositioning of the **running backs** forward, near the line position changes the **running backs** into **wide receivers**. Depending upon a play call, you may move one or both **running backs** into the **receivers** positions.

For initial instruction, have your backfield intact. Begin with your running backs in position to provide blocking protection for the QB and explain how that would work if the **tackles** were going out as **receivers**. Demonstrate these positions by placing a player in each position in the offensive formation and walk them through a running play. This is the formation from which you will conduct many of your running and passing drills. Your offensive play action calls will put the formation into its designated play plan. During these action drills, take time to refine the players actions.

Defensive Formation.

Every member of the team should know where every position in the defensive formation is located. When we consider the defensive formations basic structure, we show how the positioning of the **linebackers** to a forward, near the line position creates the position of the **outside linebacker**. This is the fundamental 4-3 defense with a **safety** back which every player should also know.

For practice, when possible, work your play actions routines against a defensive line. During these types of practices, show the defensive line how to get past the offensive line. Working both sides of the fence, so to speak. *The primary reason for understanding every position in both offense and defense is that you will have players who are playing both offense and defense.*

Blocking Practices.

The intention of a blocking practice is two fold, first to instruct the player in the proper way to block, and secondly give the player the feeling of contact in the game. Until now, most young players have not been engaged is sports which require physical contact and aggression in any way. Aggressive contact has normally been associated with an act of hostility in the youngsters thinking.

Blocking in and of itself should be done in such a way as to make it fun for the participants. In order to do that, we begin by matching the boys by like size. Not large against small, but near to each others size and weight. No boy really wants to get hurt or to hurt another boy, so keep in mind that getting good blockers is hard to come by.

In Flag Football, almost all injuries are to the down linesmen. Since no tackling is allowed, only flag pulling is permitted, the physical contact between players is primarily limited to the down linesmen. That is why it is so important to properly instruct the linesmen in the proper blocking techniques. That applies not only at the line, but when running as offense for the ball carrier.

Blocking Stance   **Blocking Engagement**

In the rules section, this is pretty much defined. The offense may contact opponents with their arms provided: The elbows are entirely outside the shoulders. The hands are closed or cupped with the palms not facing the opponent. The forearms are approximately parallel to the ground, in the same horizontal plane and extended not more than 45 degrees from the body.

The practice drill can be conducted with or without flags for the man in the backfield. Flags are preferred if possible, adding to the effect of snaring the QB. By placing several linesmen in the offensive line, the defensive linemen will attempt to get past and around the offense and grab the QB's flags. The QB may run in any direction to avoid pursuit and the offensive linemen may shift in any direction to block the defense.

The drill may be conducted with as few as two blockers and two defensive linemen. The basic objective is to get in the way of, and to contain the defense. It's not a shoving match, it's a prevent penetration drill. All members of the team will at one point or another become either an offensive lineman or a defensive lineman. This is work at the line, not running protection for a ball carrier.

Offensive line blocking practice.

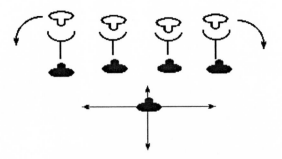

Quarterback may move in any direction to avoid being flagged except across the line.

Eventually we will work both the offensive and defensive teams into the drill as a scrimmage play. When we do that, we will have each team playing both offense and defense depending on which side has possession of the ball.

Lateral Movement Drill.

Being able to move laterally applies to both offense and defense in a game. Being able to shift quickly and move either sideways or in an oblique path requires training and practice. It applies to flag grabbing as well as blocking. Consider basketball for a moment and how much of lateral movement you see from both offense and defense during any game you attend.

During lateral movement drills, part of the drill should be practiced in the blocking mode with arms in the blockers position. The other part should be with the arms extended forward and downward to allow for grabbing of flags.

Lateral Movement Drill - all directions

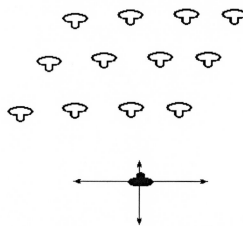

In the diagram we show moving in all directions during the drill, not just left and right. Backward movement is an important part of the drill for training your defensive backs to pick up and run with a wide receiver going past. We will cover that more closely later on.

Flag Capture Drill.

The very essence of the game! Grabbing the flags from the waist of a fleeing boy is tougher than you think. It's difficult for a youngster to grab a boy by his flags as he dashes and darts across the turf, running for his very life. As a consequence of this helter skelter foot race to escape, we must practice a method for flagging the ball carrier.

The grab for the flag should be made near the body, or even at the waistband if necessary. Attempting to grab the flag at it furthermost point outside the body is like trying to grab a fly in midair. Further from the body is the greatest amount of flutter in the flag. Once the hand has made the capture, the flag is pulled and thrown to the ground where the capture was made.

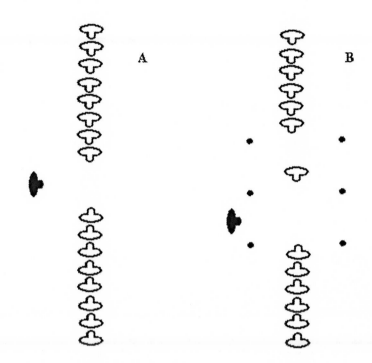

We have two simple drills which we can work with for the younger players. The simplest form is indicated as "A", and shows the team divided into two equal lines facing each other with a separation of about eight feet. The coach will toss a football to the leading player in the lower line. When the receiver grabs the ball, he must dash across the open spot towards the other line and avoid being flagged by his opponent who comes towards him.

The player in the upper line moves towards the ball carrier and makes the attempt to grab the carriers flags. Neither the ball carrier or the defensive player may run more than four feet left or right of center. The two players engaged in the effort, then continue on to the back of the opposite line and wait their next turn in the drill. Here is where you have an opportunity to instruct lateral motion by the defenseman.

This simple drill can be run while waiting to take the field for a scheduled game. It keeps the boys together, and primes them for the game.

The flag drill designated "B" will use cones to define the running area. It is conducted in the same way as drill "A", with more running room allowed, and the addition of a second defender to add pressure to the ball carrier. The use of cones to define your playing area is not only a help to you but your team. It focuses the ball carriers attention on the sidelines presence.

Capture Evasion Drill.

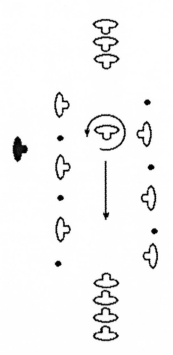

The intention of the gauntlet run is to train the ball carrier how to spin away from the defender while maintaining a forward motion. The spinning motion results in accelerating the speed of the flag adding to the difficulty of grabbing it. The movement is perfectly legal and not considered as flag guarding. The gauntlet provides two training programs into one. Flagging and avoidance.

When a player completes his run, he replaces one of the men in the gauntlet line, who in turn moves into the carriers line. Every player on the team is given a chance to experience both flagging and spinning. It is a fun drill

Running Sprint Drills.

We have no need to run the full length of the field, whether it is for 60 or 80 yards in depth. 10, 15 and 20 yards will do what we want to accomplish in sprints. One of the first things we do before sprinting drills is to stretch the legs and warm up the leg muscles. Although young muscles have elasticity and flex easily, it is still a good practice to have a warm up with plenty of stretching.

Initially, we are going to look for speed and quickness among our players. What we do in that case is to have the boys line-up abreast on a yard marker. Then on a three count they sprint to the next 10 yard marker, reverse and return to their starting yard marker. The next round have the boys line-up abreast on a yard marker. On a three count they sprint to the next 10 yard marker, reverse and return to their starting position, reverse and run to a 15 yard marker, reverse and return to their starting point.

This is the most basic of sprint drills and what we try to do is time the initial effort and try to improve on the time required to complete a running circuit. This adds a little color to an ordinary dull exercise, but it give the boys something to work against and improve their efforts without goading them into making the extra effort. You've presented a challenge.

Running Sprint Reverse Drills.

The intention of this drill is to have the runners reverse their direction and go from running forwards to running backwards until the designated yard marker is reached. By the same token, they may start by running backwards and reverse their direction into forward motion. This has special application for the defensive secondary. Being able to change from forward motion to backward direction finds application as well with the wide receivers.

We must work on improving the fluid change in direction of running in order to prevent injury and improve mobility. Consider this as an extension of the basic sprinting drills. The point of reversing direction should be at the mid-distance point between the two yard markers you have designated.

Yard Marker

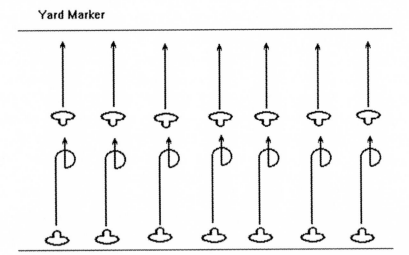

Yard Marker

Whether we select to use 10 yard markers or twenty yard markers the philosophy of reversing direction remains the same. Again, this includes all members of the team and you can again create a challenge for them by timing the effort and trying to improve on it.

Running Reverse Pickup Drills.

This drill is aimed at the **linebackers** and the **safety.** These are the players who must be able to pickup and run with an intended receiver and prevent the offensive player from getting behind them during a pass play. Don't misunderstand me that it can only apply to them, it may apply to anyone on defense.

What the defender must learn from this drill, is how close can he allow the offensive player to approach his position as he is running backwards before he must turn and run with him. In pro football, this is stressed over and over again. When any offensive player has run across the line of scrimmage, charging into the backfield, he must be picked up and covered as quickly and effectively as possible.

Defensive Linebacker & Safety Drill
Yard Marker

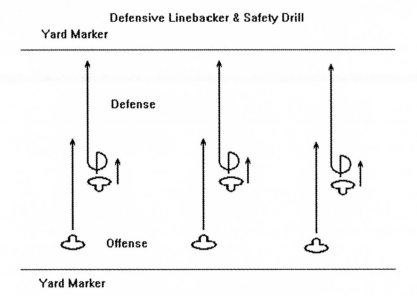

Defense

Offense

Yard Marker
Defensive Linebacker & Safety Drill

In Arena football, you have a intended receiver as the man in motion who will normally cross the line a full gallop as the ball is snapped. Boy, is that a tough one to pick up. Just remember, an offensive man in motion can cross the line at any moment the ball is snapped and if a defending lineman doesn't bump him, he's gone!

In this drill, we are looking for the player in the roll of a wide receiver to move forward to the next yard marker and try to beat the man playing defense to the line. The defender is now challenged to at least stay up with the runner. Don't mismatch the contenders in this type of effort, try keeping the playing field level in physical abilities.

The Passing Tree 3/4 Grades.

This "Tree" is coined from NFL passing plays, and is less complex than will be used by the older teams, that is grades five through eight. It does however cover the primary basics of the "Tree", and as they progress, they will move into more advanced play patterns.

Running Patterns for the Pass Play

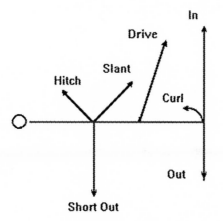

This is referred to as the "Passing Tree".

In Flag Football, everyone is an eligible receiver. That means all members of the team must have an opportunity to experience each type of passing play on the tree. Short out's and short in's are the pass staples for the Category I player. As we develop our plays later, the team will better understand how it works.

An example might be that both Wide Receivers go out from each end of the line. The left side may go short down and in while the other goes short down and out.

Practice Routes for Offensive Middle Linemen.

The Center and/or either one of both Guards are normally used for the short yardage gains. At the snap of the ball, the designated lineman receiver goes straight out, then posts up to receive the pass. Which ever of the linemen that flanked the intended receiver, must work together to close the gap created by the receiving lineman's rushing forward for the reception. Practice all three players..

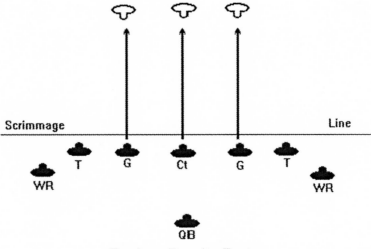

Receivers Running Routes

This is a quick play, and used when short yardage must be gained and often used to pick up the conversion points. According to the rules, One point conversion: The ball shall be placed on the 2 yard line for the attempt. Two point conversion: The ball shall be placed on the 5 yard line. Interior linemen are not considered high profile receivers and the play adds a lot of deception to the offensive game.

Practice Routes for Offensive Tackles.

Both Tackles are eligible receivers and are often involved in going out with the Wide Receiver for a double reception opportunity. Let's say that the WR on the right side is going straight out on a fly and the left Tackle is down and in. Now the QB has two options available for him to choose from, not excluding a forced run.

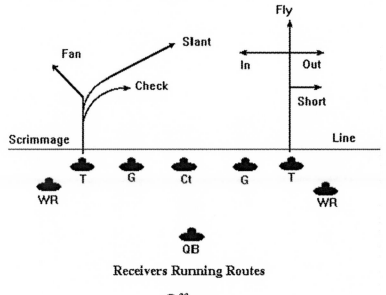

Receivers Running Routes

Offense

Regardless of the choice the QB makes, the receiver now has a blocker near enough to help him gain yardage. During our practice session, we want as many of the options run as possible. This allows the QB to get a feel for making his passing choices and to actually see the results of his efforts. When possible, have several of your players acting as **linebackers** running with the receiver on his route.

You should view the tackles as being like a tight end in regulation Football. He's and eligible receiver and also a blocker. Therefore when you put two wide receivers on one side of the line, the tackle will do what a tight end would do.

Practice Routes for Offensive Running Backs.

In flag football, when the wide receivers pull back several steps behind the line, they assume the formation features of running backs. Because running backs begin their pass routes from several steps behind the line of scrimmage, their choice of pass patterns differs slightly from those of the wide receivers.

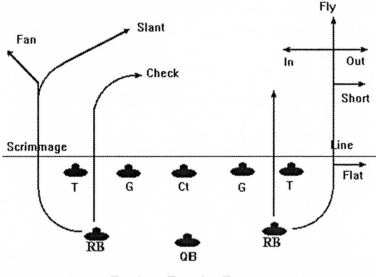

Receivers Running Routes

There are a variety of plays in which this formation will be called for. It will apply for both running and passing plays, hand-offs, laterals and flare passes which are returned to the QB for a pass downfield. It is valuable in creating deception of the intended play and throwing the defense off guard.

During practice and real games, the offensive formation may change in many ways. We will create strong side/weak side formations for sweeps and passes.

Practice Routes for Offensive Wide Receivers.

The wide receivers run all of the pass routes shown in the passing tree diagram. And those are only a partial design of the many routes that are available. In a game, these basics are expanded upon to reflect the body moves of the receiver to deceive the defensive secondary. At the level of 3/4 grades we should reduce our routes of receiver running patterns to accommodate the children's abilities.

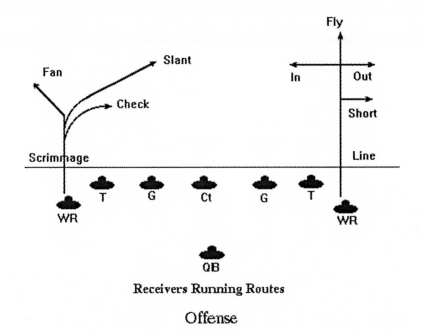

Receivers Running Routes

Offense

All receivers run patterns or routes to break free from the defenders and get open for the play. There are different distances for every route during the play, and this distance will vary with the ability of the QB to make the pass. You will have to teach your players to run for the ball, get under it. They can't expect to hit the assigned mark and stop to receive the pass. However that is what they usually do.

During our practice session, we want as many of the options run as possible. This allows the QB to get a feel for making his passing choices and to actually see the results of his efforts. When possible, have several of your players acting as **linebackers** running with the receiver on his route.

Passing Practice Summary.

Depending on the ages of your team members, some of the passing practices may be scaled down to more closely fit their abilities to perform. What is important is for all players to get an understanding of the offensive formation and how it works for the passing game. As you coach them in performance, insert your own creative concepts, don't be limited to what you find here.

Younger players from the third to the fifth grade will have trouble mastering all of this information you have to offer. However, those boys from the sixth through the eighth grades will do very well. Older players can really put these formations and concepts into practice on the playing field. All of the patterns given here are real and are put into use from high school to the NFL.

For sixth grade and above, work on spot passing, throwing to a predesignated place on the field, so the receiver runs into where the ball is being thrown and can take it on the run. If you are one of those coaches who spends time watching NFL games during the season, you may recall what is call the "West Coast Offense". That is a prime example of passing into an open spot at mid field where your wide receiver is headed as the ball is thrown.

In this chapter we included a scaled down version of the normal NFL running routes for the wide receivers and tight ends. What I want to include again in this chapter is the diagram we introduced in Chapter 8.

Running Patterns for the Pass Play

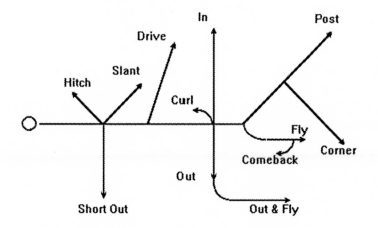

This is referred to as the "Passing Tree".

This is the set of routes you are most familiar with from you experience in coaching football. They apply to either left handed or right handed play patterns.

Chapter 11

Practice Planning Schedule.

It all begins with the amount of time allocated to the sports program by either the school, YMCA, Youth Foundation, Parks and Recreations Sport Office, Inner City Athletics, etc.. Depending on the categories of your players, you may be given a game schedule from eight to twelve or more weeks.

This begins a string of questions you will have to deal with. What is the amount of time allowed for a practice session, and how many sessions may you have per week? How much practice will there be prior to your first game? Considering the age and ability of your team and its players, how much can you reasonably accomplish before your first game?

How do you start planning your practices? That is based upon the facilities available to you and their times of availability. It is also based upon the availability of your team members. It can't be during school hours, so it must be after school. Most of the fields will be closed to practice on the weekends because that is normally when they will have scheduled games. However you do have a preseason period which may change some of those restrictions in your favor.

I suggest that you plan your practices right after school or during the early evening. Avoid late evening practices if possible. Schedule your practice time on any day Monday through Friday. For some of you, there may be Sunday practices if facilities are available. If no park fields are available, you may be able to use the ones at your local schools.

When you are coaching young players, the earlier in the evening the better for them. There is also the consideration of when the parents are able to bring the kids to practice. In formulating the practice schedule you have to take into account all of the factors which comprise the team as a whole. That is the availability of yourself, the players and the parents along with the facility.

Use a practice scrimmage among your team players and attempt to assess their weakness' and their strengths. Based upon your observation you will be able to determine the type of instruction to be given. For the most part, your younger players will require the greatest amount of time in the basics.

When you prioritize the players needs in training, be realistic. Keep an honest perspective of what can and cannot be achieved with a limited amount of practice and training time. Refrain from having expectations that are beyond the abilities of the kids. Don't be intimidated by the game schedule. Set a steady learning pace for the team and let the win or loss of a game become secondary.

Make a chart. The left hand side or column represents your time frame. On the right side place the exercises or drills you want to have the players practice. As you progress with your training program, you will begin removing some of the earlier exercises and replacing them with new ones. Follow your plan. Obtain your teams training goals and their success.

As a general example, let's assume we can have a one hour practice session once or twice a week. How do you make something happen during such a short period of time? We start by breaking down the one hour into segments.

Allow the first ten minutes to be their passing and receiving warm up drills. For the youngest of players, set the passing distance at about 10 yards. Half way through, increase the distance by 5 feet. With older players, start at 10 yards and increase the distance in increments of 5 yards until you have a good handle on 30 yards.

Have the team, all members, form into three lines. Have the Quarter Back and both Wide Receivers act as the passers.

Take the next thirty minutes for offense and defensive instructions on where the player assignments are and how each assignment functions during game play. This covers the interior line and the backs as well as the defensive front four and the linebackers.

Take the remainder of your time for game practice allowing the kids to have fun with the game. Let your players scrimmage, the offense against the defense. Allow them to call their own plays, or create the plays they want to run. To add another dimension to the play, have them play a mock game against each other.

There are only six basic skills to be taught. Passing, receiving, blocking, lateral movements, running and kicking. Each skill requires instruction and practice by every member of the team. Playing a given team position brings with it a certain type of skill requirements which must be learned during drills and practices.

As the coach, you will be required to demonstrate all of the skills that a player must acquire in order to play this game. Make sure you can get their attention whenever you show them how to do what it is you want them to do. Make it fun and use your sense of humor. Each skill has its very own way of being performed, and that is your job to teach.

I suggest that you make 3 x 5 cards with your action plays drawn on them. Show the team the card that has their practice play outlined on it and explain to them what each player is to do. When they see their assignments prior to the play, they are most apt to perform the way you want them to. This is a visual reinforcement of what you want them to do, it's the plan!

These cards work for both offense and defense. When you are coaching the defense team show them your 3 x 5 card with their defensive positions outlined. Let them know it is a 4-3 or a 3-4 defense formation so you may call for either one as you need. Don't forget to make cards for blitz and dog formations.

Category I is third and fourth graders playing with a coach on the field during a game.. Schedule in at least a one hour or more practice session per week. Normally these youngsters will be scheduled for their games during the week beginning at 6:00 p.m..

If you are scheduled for a Saturday game, arrange your practice on either Wednesday, Thursday or Friday. I shouldn't have to tell you that, but I am going to anyway and the reasons are obvious. More of the practice session will be retained and used by the players than if they have had a longer layoff. The fresher the practice session, the better the game. The better they play, the better they feel and the better job you are doing.

Select your practice drills from chapter 10, or be creative and devise a few of your very own. You can do that! You must also include the offensive team formations you will be using during games to be played. At the **Category I** level I keep action plays very simple, with two running plays and two passing plays. Since action plays are left and right handed, I have instead of four plays, I have eight.

These are divided by using two different offensive formations which you may select or devise yourself. Let's say we use the shotgun and the spread formations. They are easy to remember and easy to operate from. Make sure that your team gets to see an outline of the plays in action and who is doing what.

Category II is a whole new ball game for these kids. We now have 5th and 6th grade players

I suggest that you schedule at least two practice sessions a week regardless of the games played. You will have practice and league games which will be split between Saturdays and week nights. The practice session should be one hour or more if possible.

Allow the first ten minutes to be their passing and receiving warm up drills. For these players, set the passing distance at about 10 yards. Increase the distance in increments of 5 yards until you have a good handle on 30 yards.

Have the team, all members, form into three lines. Have the Quarter Back and both Wide Receivers act as the passers.

Take the next thirty minutes for offense and defensive instructions on where the player assignments are and how each assignment functions during game play. This covers the interior line and the backs as well as the defensive front four and the linebackers. Work hard on the running plays with the offensive line running with the ball carrier. The passing plays must be clearly defined and their receiving patterns established. Use the passing tree and running trees to help you set the team in motion.

Take the remainder of your time for game practice allowing the kids to have fun with the game. Let your players scrimmage, the offense against the defense. Allow them to call their own plays, or create the plays they want to run. To add another dimension to the play, have them play a mock game against each other.

These players are capable of performing all of the basics pretty well. Your guide lines will be more detailed and directed than in the previous practice session. You should be teaching them your set plays which will be signaled from the side lines or carried on field by an alternate player.

Select your practice drills from chapter 10, or be creative and devise a few of your very own. You can do that! You must also include the offensive team formations you will be using during games to be played. At the **Category II** level I keep action plays simple, with four running plays and four passing plays. Since action plays are left and right handed, I have instead of eight plays, I have sixteen.

These are divided by using four different offensive formations which you may select or devise yourself. Let's say we use the shotgun, spread, slot and single wing formations. They are easy to remember and easy to operate from. Make sure that your team gets to see an outline of the plays in action and who is doing what.

It's a good idea to make copies of your action plays and pass them out among the team members. Include your offensive and defensive action sheets so every member knows exactly what is going on. We use these during our training drills as our guide lines. You must cover two or more of these plays at each and every session.

Category III is a new step up for everyone involved. 7th & 8th grade players are big strong boys. Much more mature and a great deal more fun than the younger athletes. This age group laughs more with each other, and doesn't lose their tempers as often.

Players in this age group have a strong tendency to emulate the other players on the team who are better players and learn from them. They quickly pick up from each other, so that you don't have to concentrate on basics as you must with the younger players. They are also more interested in helping each other become better. As a result, your better players will always help the less skilled players to improve without you making a point of it.

This is where hustle begins and just playing ends. I suggest that you schedule at least two practice sessions a week regardless of the games played. You will have practice and league games which will be split between Saturdays and week nights. The practice session should be no less than one hour and more if possible.

Allow the first ten minutes to be their passing and receiving warm up drills. For these players, set the passing distance at about 10 yards. Increase the distance in increments of 5 yards until you have a good handle on 30 yards.

Have the team, all members, form into three lines. Have the Quarter Back and both Wide Receivers act as the passers. Have them running hitches and comebacks.

Take the next thirty minutes for offense and defensive instructions on where the player assignments are and how each assignment functions during game play. This covers the interior line and the backs as well as the defensive front four and the linebackers. Work hard on the running plays with the offensive line running with the ball carrier. The passing plays must be clearly defined and their receiving patterns established. Use the passing tree and running trees to help you set the team in motion.

Take the remainder of your time for game practice allowing the kids to have fun with the game. Let your players scrimmage, the offense against the defense. Allow them to call their own plays, or create the plays they want to run. To add another dimension to the play, have them play a mock game against each other.

Select your practice drills from chapter 10, or be creative and devise a few of your very own. You can do that! You must also include the offensive team formations you will be using during games to be played. At the **Category** III level, the action plays become more complex, with four running plays and eight passing plays. Since action plays are left and right handed, I have instead of twelve plays, I have twenty four.

These are divided by using four different offensive formations which you may select or devise yourself. Let's say we use the shotgun, spread, slot and single wing formations. They are easy to remember and easy to operate from. Make sure that your team gets to see an outline of the plays in action and who is doing what.

How does that work? The same way it does in regulation football where the basic formation begins to generate a wide variety of plays with multiple options among the receivers running routes, and who the receivers are to be. Once you begin to generate your play action patterns from a basic formation, the ideas will pour like rain off a roof.

It's a good idea to make copies of your action plays and pass them out among the team members. Include your offensive and defensive action sheets so every member knows exactly what is going on. We use these during our training drills as our guide lines. You must cover two or more of these plays at each and every session.

Chapter 12

COACHING THE GAME

Category I. For boys in grades 3 & 4 divisions the playing area is sixty yards, divided into three, 20 yard zones. The end zones are 10 yards in depth The width shall be 40 yards, space permitting.

3 / 4 Grades Playing Field

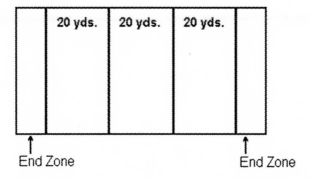

Kicking team shall kickoff from the 20 yard line in the 3/4 grade division. This line will act as the kickoff teams restraining line. The midfield line shall act as the restraining line for the receiving team.

On kickoff. the kicking team may use any formation as long as the entire team is behind their restraining line and in bounds. The receiving team may use any formation as long as the entire team is behind their restraining line and at least 3 players are within five yards of the restraining line.

Player Positions

Offense: (8) Players.

Offensive Line: T= (2)Tackle G= (2)Guard Ct= Center

Backfield: WR= (2)Wide Receiver/Tight End QB=Quarterback

Defense: (8) Players.

Defensive Line: DE= (2) Defensive Ends DG= (2) Defensive Guards

Defensive Backfield: LB= (2/3) Line Backers Sf= (1/2) Safety or Cornerbacks.

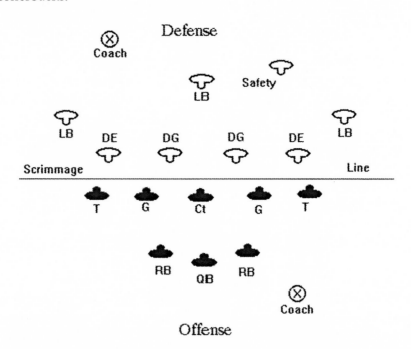

In this diagram we show both the defensive and offensive formations with a coach on the field with his team. The offensive coach will conduct the huddle to instruct his team in how to make the next play, at the

same time he is training the team that all must come to the huddle before the next play is activated.

The coach is also allowed to place his players in their correct positions prior to the snap call. During defense, the coach teaches how to avoid encroachment and not to get a penalty. On offense he must train his team not to make a false start prior to the snap. Off-side calls are common at this young age level, but they get the hang of it quickly.

The coach must stay out of the way of play and out of the referees way when action is taking place. During the play action you do not instruct individuals on your team as to what to do. Instruction is given after a play is made, and given to the engaged team as a whole. Always build on what was done well.

Recriminations suck! Don't call your huddle and in front of all the players, berate a member of the team for what he didn't do. Just tell the boys what they did well and what you want to see them do on the next play. You may have a play called "run-right-run" for a running sweep around right end. What happens? The scramble is on at the snap of the ball and the running back goes left. Oh, well.

I suggest that you make 3 x 5 cards with your action plays drawn on them. Show the team the card that has their next play outlined on it and explain to them what each player is to do. When they see their assignments prior to the play, they are most apt to perform the way you want them to. You have also lifted the pressure off each player from having to remember the details of a play you may have done in practice.

These cards work for both offense and defense. When you coach the defending team, you verbally place the boys in their positions as you read the offense. After the play is completed, quick huddle the boys and show them your 3 x 5 card with their defensive positions outlined. Let them know it was a 4-3 or a 3-4 defense so you may call for that set-up again.

You will also have show cards for your kickoff, punting, kick returns and special teams. As you get into the season, the team will have begun to remember more and more of your formation instructions. Now is when the fun begins for them and you. The coaching audible is quickly followed by formation alignment. The team will take pride in itself because it has the power of knowledge.

Player rotation in most other sports can be a pain in selecting who should be in the game and who should not. In Flag Football we have a place for every single player on the team. And every player will play almost half of every game. It's simple, we have the offensive unit and the defensive unit. Different boys will prefer one to the other, and some will never want to come off of the field.

It pretty well works out that some boys will play almost the entire game because they play both offense and defense. Some will only want to play defense and sack the quarterback or grab the flags. The team will crossover from offense to defense and beg for the chance to do exactly that.

Category II. For boys in grades 5 & 6 divisions the playing area is eighty yards, divided into four, 20 yard zones. The end zones are 10 yards in depth The width shall be 40 yards, space permitting.

The new field dimensions adds a lot of room for the teams to cover at a run. The addition of twenty yards to the field adds to the length of the game and to the difficulty in scoring. The number of balls being punted on the field doubles. Kickoff returns seldom result in a scoring run to the kicking teams end zone.

Kicking team shall kickoff from the 30 yard line in the 5/6 grade division. This line will act as the kickoff teams restraining line. The midfield line shall act as the restraining line for the receiving team.

On kickoff. the kicking team may use any formation as long as the entire team is behind their restraining line and in bounds. The receiving team may use any formation as long as the entire team is behind their restraining line and at least 3 players are within five yards of the restraining line.

Grades 5 - 8 Playing Field Layout

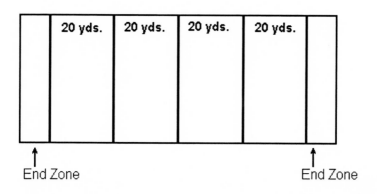

End Zone   End Zone

At the level of the 5th and 6th grade players and above, no coach is allowed on the field except during a called time-out. It's different than what you experienced when coaching the third and fourth grade teams. Again, I would suggest that you make 3 x 5 cards with your action plays drawn on them.

I retain an alternate back or wide receiver on the sidelines with me in order to carry the next offensive play into the huddle. How that works is when an offensive play has just ended with the ball being called dead. The receiver or back nearest to my side of the sidelines will come off the field and his replacement is then sent in.

Before the replacement leaves me, I show him the 3 x 5 action play card and what I want the next play to be. By showing him the card before he goes onto the field, the diagram will remain clear in his mind. Sometimes that magic doesn't work. But for the most part it works in a game. His job is to take the play call into the huddle with the QB.

Player rotation in Flag Football is no problem, we have a place for every single player on the team. And every player will play almost half of every game. It's simple, we have the offensive unit and the defensive unit. Different boys will prefer one to the other, and some will never want to come off of the field.

It pretty well works out that some boys will play almost the entire game because they play both offense and defense. Some will only want to play defense and sack the quarterback or grab the flags.

In the illustration we show sixteen positions filled by the team. It is easy enough to see how we can spread individual participation across the playing time requirements. Most of the teams which I have had or played against, never had more than fifteen players. And regardless of how challenged a youngster was by lack of ability or over weight as an example, they all played in every quarter.

When we are coaching boys in this age group, they are fairly competent at running passing routes and handling the ball. Therefore, we have the ability and the desire to run more passing plays than running plays. Although I have as many running options as passing plays, I tend to call for more passing plays than running plays. The team likes that better also.

How about defense? The middle linebacker will be responsible to spread his men to set up his defensive formation. You can send him a hand signal to indicate a 4-3 or a 3-4, a blitz or a dog. Or, you allow him to make those decisions on his own. Within a few games, he'll be more than capable for setting up his formation by himself. If things are not going well with defense, call a time-out and huddle the team for your instructions.

It's not as important for the defensive middle linemen to be large as it is for the offensive down linesmen. What I always look for is the aggressive and quick players to get through the line and into the other teams backfield. The outside linebackers may be larger and fast to force the end run back towards the middle.

In the past, my defensive unit has won the games for the team. If the other team can't score, they can't beat us! Our most successful formation has been the 4-3 or 4-4 to not only close down the running play, but make a lot of interceptions. The middle linebacker acts upon the offense more than he reacts to it. Once he reads the offensive formation, he will shift the defensive formation to match it.

Category III. For boys in grades 7 & 8 divisions the playing area is eighty yards, divided into four, 20 yard zones. The end zones are 10 yards in depth The width shall be 40 yards, space permitting.

Kicking team shall kickoff from the 30 yard line in the 7/8 grade division. This line will act as the kickoff teams restraining line. The midfield line shall act as the restraining line for the receiving team.

On kickoff. the kicking team may use any formation as long as the entire team is behind their restraining line and in bounds. The receiving team may use any formation as long as the entire team is behind their restraining line and at least 3 players are within five yards of the restraining line.

No coach is allowed on the field except during a called time-out. Again, I would suggest that you make 3 x 5 cards with your action plays drawn on them.

During the game, I retain an alternate back or wide receiver on the sidelines with me in order to carry the next offensive play into the huddle. How that works is when an offensive play has just ended with the ball being called dead. The receiver or back nearest to my side of the sidelines will come off the field and his replacement is then sent in.

Before the replacement leaves me, I show him the 3 x 5 action play card and what I want the next play to be. By showing him the card before he goes onto the field, the diagram will remain clear in his mind. His job is to take the play call into the huddle with the QB and team.

Player rotation in Flag Football is no problem, we have a place for every single player on the team. We have sixteen positions to be filled by the team. It is easy enough to see how we can spread individual participation across the playing time requirements. Most of the teams which I have had or played against, never had more than fifteen players. And regardless of how challenged a youngster was by lack of ability or over weight as an example, they all played in every quarter.

When we are coaching boys in this age group, they are fairly competent at running passing routes and handling the ball. Therefore, we have the ability and the desire to run more passing plays than running plays. As a matter of fact, if you refer back to Chapter 11, the team will have twice as many passing plays as running plays. Running plays are hard to make in this division.

How about defense? The middle linebacker will be responsible to spread his men to set up his defensive formation. You can send him a hand signal to indicate a 4-3 or a 3-4, a blitz or a dog. Or, you allow him to make those decisions on his own. Within a few games, he'll be more than capable for setting up his formation by himself. If things are not going well with defense, call a time-out and huddle the team for your instructions.

It's not as important for the defensive middle linemen to be large as it is for the offensive down linesmen. What I always look for is the aggressive and quick players to get through the line and into the other teams backfield. The outside linebackers may be larger and fast to force the end run back towards the middle.

In the past, my defensive unit has won the games for the team. If the other team can't score, they can't beat us! Our most successful formation has been the 4-3 or 4-4 to not only close down the running play, but make a lot of interceptions. The middle linebacker acts upon the offense more than he reacts to it. Once he reads the offensive formation, he will shift the defensive formation to match it. And when the ball is snapped the action is on.

What I want in the defensive backfield are my taller players who may have a height advantage over the intended receiver during a passing play. We always want the taller, faster and quicker player with good hands to out perform and to intercept the ball. Just part of the wish list I guess. You will now discover that most of your time-outs will be with the defensive unit.

As we mentioned earlier, we will have twice as many passing plays as we will have running plays. One thing about the passing play is to give the quarterback the option of having two receivers on their running routes. He is then able to make a quick assessment of an open receiver, if there is an open receiver, or option to run.

Quickness of performance is everything at the 7th & 8th grade levels of play. These players have new bodies that are pumping adult hormones. They are strong and quick and aggressive. They also have what we have all had, growing pains. Expect some of your taller kids to have complaints about leg and lower body pains.

The team will now have more injuries than before, which are hits and bruises. When a boy gets hurt, don't allow him to reenter the game until you are sure he is okay. Observe closely what is taking place at the line with and against the opposing team. If one of your players is losing his temper, pull him out and cool him down. Also look for late blocking hits by your team and the opponents team.

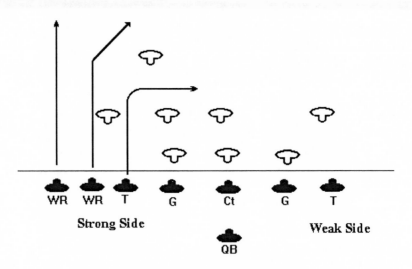

Offensive Option Formation

Lets look at left handed and right handed plays before we quit.

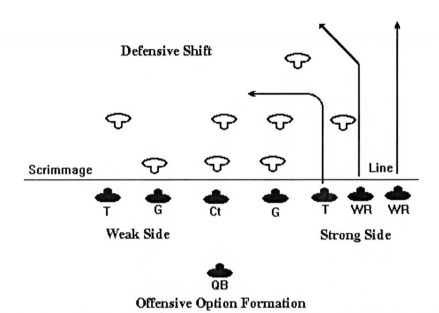

Defensive Shift

Scrimmage   Line

T   G   Ct   G   T   WR   WR

Weak Side   **Strong Side**

QB
Offensive Option Formation

When we are designing our plays, this is how they are going to look on your cards that we have discussed. So, every time you design an action play, you automatically generate the flip side of the play. That is why you can generate dozens of easy plays from a single basic formation.

I had mentioned earlier about letting members of your team design an action play. Let all of the boys have a chance to come up with some new and wonderful idea. This really brings focus on preset plays you have given them. I've had so many youngsters approach me with an idea for a play that I had not thought of for that team. I was impressed by how much the kids want to be a part of the decision making process.

One last thought on coaching the team during a game. If the team is doing well at all, allow the quarterback to take over the offensive unit and call the play he wants to call. When I want the quarterback to take charge, I signal from the sidelines with both thumbs up. Now what will normally happen is the backfield will decide the play by committee. It just happens that way.

My intention is to create total involvement with the game and its outcome with every member of the team <u>by turning as much control over to them as they can handle.</u> That does not mean that I step away from it, because I don't. If offense falters, I call a time-out huddle and start from scratch all over again by sending in the plays from the sidelines. <u>You would be surprised how well the members will police themselves to play better.</u>

Chapter 13

WARM UP DRILLS:

The warm up drills are intended to exercise the body in such a way as to compliment the practice drills. Muscles and ligaments used during practice and play should be stretched and warmed before active drills are run. What we are interested in here is the ham string, Achilles tendon, lower back and upper shoulders.

Those drills listed below are only a few of the many possibilities now available to you. Employ as many other or different ones as you are familiar with, and use them judiciously. Category I requires the less strenuous exercises. Beyond that, please expand freely, but do not turn an exercise into an ordeal.

Circuit Jogging - Warm-up No. 1.

This is not a race. Slow jog the perimeter of the field, shaking out the arms and hands. This is intended to be a loosening up jog. Get the blood flowing and the entire body warmed up. The number of circuits will depend on the children's ages and conditions. Don't make it an ordeal, it's just a simple warm-up that you can start or finish with.

Waist, Torso & Upper Body - Warm-up No. 2.

Form the players into two lines that face you from left to right and two players deep. Have them spread out sideways until their fingers cannot touch.

Have them spread their feet shoulder width facing you. On the first count with arms extended at shoulder height sideways , have them twist their torso to face their upper bodies to the left.

Second count returns them to facing you, the third count have them twist their torso to face their upper bodies to the right. Fourth count returns them to facing forward again. Do twelve cycles.

Waist, Torso & Upper Body - Warm-up No. 3.

Form the players into two lines that face you from left to right and two players deep. Have them spread out sideways until their fingers cannot touch. Have them spread their feet shoulder width facing you. On the first count with hands on their hips, have them bend forward and reach for their toes.

Second count returns them upright to facing you, on the third count have them bend their upper bodies backwards. Fourth count returns them to upright facing forward again. Do twelve cycles.

Vertical Body Stretch and Calf - Warm-up No. 4.

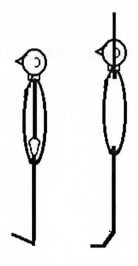

Form the players into two lines that face you from left to right and two players deep. Have them spread out sideways until their fingers cannot touch. Have them spread their feet slightly apart and hands at their sides facing you.

On the first count rock backwards on the heels while lifting the toes from the ground. Second count rocks them forward onto their toes and up as they raise their hands and arms reaching for the sky. The third count returns them to their starting position. Do twelve cycles.

Vertical Body Stretch and Side - Warm-up No. 5.

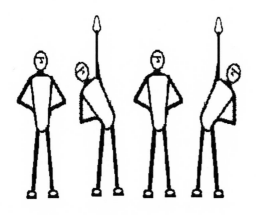

Form the players into two lines that face you from left to right and two players deep. Have them spread out sideways until their fingers cannot touch. Have them spread their feet shoulder width and hands on their hips facing you.

On the first count raise their left hand reaching for the sky and bending to their right side. Second count returns them to the start position. Third count raise their right hand reaching for the sky and bending to their left side. Fourth count returns them to the start position. Do twelve cycles.

Leg Lunge and Quadriceps - Warm-up No. 6.

Form the players into three lines. Each line will follow the person at the head of the line. With their back straight, step forward with the right foot, plant the foot and lower the body until the left knee touches the ground. Hold a moment then push back to the up position and pull the left foot even with the right.

With their back straight, step forward with the left foot, plant the foot and lower the body until the right knee touches the ground. Hold a moment then push back to the up position and pull the right foot even with the left.

Continue the exercise until the players have crossed the width of the diamond. This is not a hurry up exercise, take your time. Some of the small players may have difficulty, if so, shorten the length of the training path.

Leg Squats and Quadriceps - Warm-up No. 7.

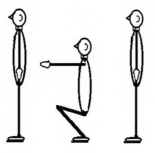

Form the players into two lines that face you from left to right and two players deep. Have them spread out sideways until their fingers cannot touch. Have them spread their feet shoulder width and hands on their hips facing you. On the first count have them squat with arms forward , outstretched for balance until the legs are folded. Second count returns them to their original position. Do twelve cycles.

Side Straddle Hop - Warm-up No. 8.

Form the players into two lines that face you from left to right and two players deep. Have them spread out sideways until their fingers cannot touch. Have them place their feet together and hands at their sides facing you. On the count of one, they must jump vertically, spreading their feet and raising their hands overhead to clap. On the second count they return to their starting position. You may use a two count or four count cadence.

Vertical Jump - Warm-up No. 9.

Form the players into two lines that face you from left to right and two players deep. Have them spread out sideways until their fingers cannot touch. What we want is to have the players jump as high with arms going up on the jump as they can reach. The cadence is jump, bounce, bounce, jump, bounce, bounce. The bounce is a short vertical jump above ankle high.

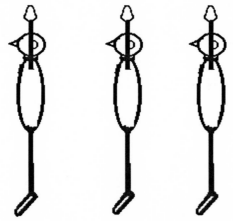

Biography

A writer and author. Life long involvement in sports as a participant and for more than thirty years a volunteer coach. I have trained many new coaches in how to do planning, scheduling and rotation of players during practices and games. Teaching how to coax the best from players. The tenure has covered baseball, basketball, football, tennis and wrestling.

0-595-22523-3

Printed in the United States
87123LV00004B/328-330/A